PRAISE FOR *SUPERPOWER!*

"Ford Saeks is an international expert on all matters marketing and branding. In this book he shares solid ideas and practical strategies to build your business and enhance your life."

— **Dr. Nido R. Qubein, President, High Point University**

"This amazing book is loaded with practical, proven strategies that you can use immediately to get what you want in every area of your life."

— **Brian Tracy, CEO, Brian Tracy International Inc.**

"You will not find a better marketing person on the planet than Ford Saeks."

— **Michael Hudson, Credit Union Strategies**

"Having booked Ford for multiple franchise events over the years, our franchise brands love Superpower! because it is relevant to new franchisees, multi-unit owners, and producers looking for ways to elevate their mindset and take personal accountability for their own results."

— **Katrina Mitchell, Chief Match Maker, Franchise Speakers**

"We like using *Superpower!* as a gift for new commercial customers because we understand that any size organization can benefit from improving their leadership and personal performance."

— **Chad Hoffman, CEO, Richwood Bank**

"In today's fast-paced environment where people easily get overwhelmed with multiple priorities and demands, it's nice to have *Superpower!* as a guide to help us engage and retain our staff and customers."

— **Carrie Burrell, VP Marketing Manager, Mission Valley Bank**

"Many factors go into franchise success, with developing a positive mindset being the foundation. Superpower! is measurable and authentic and speaks to the challenges facing today's organizations. It has filled that gap for our family of franchises. Thanks, Ford!"

— **Becky Bongiovanni, Brand President, CarePatrol Franchise Systems, LLC**

"This book is what everyone needs today if they are going to succeed. The new economic realities dictate that we must change the mindsets from which we operate. If you want to be at the top of your game and enjoy life the way you want it to be, you need to read SUPERPOWER! You can bet your competition is reading it too."

— **Ron Karr, author of *Lead, Sell or Get Out of the Way***

"Ford Saeks has achieved great success by working smart and working hard, and he shows you how to get things done, faster and easier."

— **Brian Foster, CEO, United Sports Solutions, Inc.**

"Ford has overcome tough odds to achieve great success by working smart and working hard. This book shows you how he did it and how you can do it, too. He'll help you achieve superpower, not through magic or gimmicks, but by using his proven strategies and tactics. Read it if you want super results."

— **Mark Sanborn, acclaimed speaker and best-selling author of *The Fred Factor* and *You Don't Need a Title to Be a Leader***

"Everybody has the ability to be extraordinary...everybody. Ford Saeks has discovered how to unleash the overlooked power available to you. He's done it in his own amazing life and can show you how to do the same. Activate your Superpower before another minute of extraordinary living passes you by."

— Jim Cathcart, author of
***The Acrorn Principle*, Hall of Fame Professional Speaker**

"Ford Saeks has the experience, insights, and unique perspective to show you how to become a SUPERPOWER. This book is a must-read today, as tomorrow your competitors will have it!"

— Sam Silverstein, founder, The Accountability Academy

"Ford Saeks is a brilliant thought leader in the world of personal and professional success. Follow the steps in this book, and you will prosper in all areas of your life"

— Shep Hyken, New York Times best-selling author of
The Amazement Revolution

"Wouldn't it be great if you had a guide to help you be your most incredible self? You have it right here. With his straight talk and common-sense approach, Ford Saeks makes the process easy, intuitive, and, most of all, effective. This book will help get you where you want to be.""

— Victoria Labalme, CEO,
Victoria Labalme Communications, LLO

"Ford's book, Superpower! helped me and my team improve the way we approach challenges, make course corrections, and is filled with practical insights that can be applied to any organization. I'm a CEO of a company that's all over the globe, and I travel a lot, so I don't have any time to waste. He tells it like it is, without the fluff, in easy to consume and implement language. Get a copy for everyone on your team."

— Sean Engbrecht, CEO, CASS Global Security

SUPERPOWER!

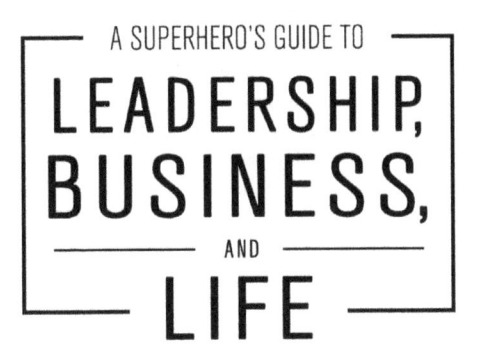

A SUPERHERO'S GUIDE TO
LEADERSHIP, BUSINESS, AND LIFE

FORD SAEKS

PRIMECONCEPTS
PRESS

A DIVISION OF PRIME CONCEPTS GROUP, INC.

Copyright © 2012–2022 by Ford Saeks, Prime Concepts Group, Inc. All rights reserved.

Published by Prime Concepts Group Press. A division of Prime Concepts Group, Inc.

No part of this publication may be reproduced, stored in a retrieval system, or transmitted in any form or by any means, electronic, mechanical, photocopying, recording, scanning, or otherwise, except as permitted under Section 107 or 108 of the 1976 United States Copyright Act, without either the prior written permission of the Publisher. Requests to the Publisher for permission should be addressed to Prime Concepts Group Inc., 115 S. Hydraulic St, Wichita, KS 67211

Limit of Liability/Disclaimer of Warranty: While the publisher and author have used their best efforts in preparing this book, they make no representations or warranties with respect to the accuracy or completeness of the contents of this book and specifically disclaim any implied warranties of merchantability or fitness for a particular purpose. No warranty may be created or extended by sales representatives or written sales materials. The advice and strategies contained herein may not be suitable for your situation. You should consult with a professional where appropriate. Neither the publisher nor author shall be liable for any loss of profit or any other commercial damages, including but not limited to special, incidental, consequential, or other damages.

For volume book purchases, speaking, media interviews or book signings, please contact Profit Rich Results at ProfitRichResults.com or call 1-316-844-0235

For general information on our creative agency services contact us through PrimeConcepts.com or call 1-316-942-1111

Prime Concepts Group Press publishes in a variety of print and electronic formats and by print-on-demand. Some material included with standard print versions of this book may not be included in e-books, audio, or in print-on-demand.

Saeks, Ford, 1961 –
Superpower! The Superhero's Guide to Leadership, Business, and Life / Ford Saeks
p. cm.

Hardback ISBN: 978-1-884667-45-9
Paperback ISBN: 978-1-884667-43-5
Kindle Version ISBN: 978-1-884667-44-2
Success 2. Success in Business. 3 Self-actualization
LCCN: 9781884667435
Printed in the United States of America

CONTENTS

Congratulations, You Have Superpowers. Now What?

Superpower! is a guidebook for taking personal accountability of your success. That's where all the power and responsibility is — within you. Think of it as a handbook with stories and steps to help you rethink, reframe, refocus, and reignite your leadership, your business, and your life. The strategies and tactics offered here are like tools. Not every tool is right for every job. Choose the ones that are right for you and your situation. I've included a variety of scenarios. The idea is to help you develop a diverse set of skills so you can arm yourself with an arsenal of superpowers, helping you bridge the gap between where you are today and where you want to be.

INTRODUCTION	1
PART 1:	
RETHINK	5
CHAPTER ONE: THE BIRTH OF A SUPERHERO	7
CHAPTER TWO: CREATING THE SUPERHERO MINDSET	25
CHAPTER THREE: THE SUPERPOWER OF PROSPERITY CONSCIOUSNESS	35
CHAPTER FOUR: SUPER SENSE	51
PART 2:	
REFRAME	61
CHAPTER FIVE: SUCCESS-RAY VISION	63
CHAPTER SIX: ADDING VALUE IS A SUPERPOWER	73
CHAPTER SEVEN: THE POWER OF IDEAS	79
CHAPTER EIGHT: CRITICAL THINKING: USING YOUR SUPER SMARTS	89

PART 3:
REFOCUS
95

CHAPTER NINE: THE SUPER STRENGTH OF INTUITION — 97
CHAPTER TEN: SUPERHUMAN SIMPLICITY — 101
CHAPTER ELEVEN: THE POWER OF MONOTASKING — 107

PART 4:
REIGNITE
115

CHAPTER TWELVE: UP, UP AND AWAY — 117
CHAPTER THIRTEEN: BULLETPROOF TIME MANAGEMENT — 127
CHAPTER FOURTEEN: MENTORSHIP MAGIC — 135
CHAPTER FIFTEEN: THE POWER OF GRATITUDE — 145

PART 5:
REFLECT
153

CHAPTER SIXTEEN: THE POWER TO PIVOT — 155
CHAPTER SEVENTEEN: SUPERPOWERED REFLEXES — 163
CHAPTER EIGHTEEN: CREATING YOUR CAST OF CHARACTERS — 173

PART 6:
REWARD
177

CHAPTER NINETEEN: CELEBRATE YOUR WINS — 179
CHAPTER TWENTY: POWERFUL RESULTS — 185

ABOUT THE AUTHOR — 187
CONNECT WITH FORD ONLINE — 189
WATCH FORD'S SPEAKER TRAILER — 194
DOWNLOAD THE HERO HANDBOOK — 195
INDEX — 196

DOWNLOAD THE HERO HANDBOOK

Superpowerbook.com/downloads

The Hero Handbook will help you take personal accountability for your success. That's where all the power and responsibility is — within you.

Download and print your Hero Handbook-then write answers to the questions and action steps at the end of each chapter, and use this handbook as your guide to elevating your leadership, business, and personal life habits.

INTRODUCTION

Most people skip the acknowledgments pages. I'm going to challenge you to read mine because it explains why I wrote this book in the first place.

This book is a compilation of strategies, tactics, ideas, and concepts that I've used throughout my life on my journey of success and fulfillment. Some of these ideas may sound familiar, while others may sound outrageous. Every effort has been made to give credit to other authors or thought leaders for their contribution to my success in the strategies. You see, I've been on the road of personal growth and development for more than 40 years. I've read countless books, listened to countless audiobooks, and attended hundreds of seminars on a wide variety of topics.

As a renowned business growth accelerator and hall of fame keynote speaker (you can discover more about that at ProfitRichResults.com), I've presented to hundreds of thousands of people from organizations around the globe on a variety of business-related and success topics. Those topics include developing a superpower mindset, accelerating business growth, and creating a culture of leadership excellence.

As a consultant, I've worked with hundreds of top brands of all sizes to help them find, attract, and keep their customers; increase the performance of their teams; and increase their sales and profits. That process always starts with evaluating where people and organizations are now, identifying where they want to go, and then developing the strategic plan and specific action steps to reach their goals. Working through this process repeatedly, applying different strategies, and making adjustments and course corrections have given me unique insights into how top performers think.

My goal for this book is to give you and the people you care about insights on using your superpower. My definition of superpower is simple: **the ability to expand your critical thinking skills, take action, and produce the results you desire in your life.**

I've been an entrepreneur since I was 12 years old. I listened to my first motivational cassette program while I was in a detention center for at-risk youths. It was those words of positive encouragement and new ideas that expanded my thinking and put me on the path to success. Over the years, I've founded and grown multiple companies, and I've been responsible for hundreds of employees. I've sought out experts who've done what I wanted to do, so I could learn from them, model their behavior, and produce similar or even better results. To acknowledge every single person who helped me along the way would fill an entire shelf of books, even if I could remember all of their names, which I can't.

However, one person I'd like to thank is my wife, Aliesa George. Aliesa has believed in me at those times when I doubted my own success. It was through her love and encouragement, and our many late-night mastermind sessions, that this book concept was born. She deserves credit for formulating the outline and for helping me capture these strategies and put them into a readable format. She is a successful entrepreneur in her own right(Centerworks.com), and I couldn't ask for a better friend, soul mate, sounding board, and life partner.

Special thanks go out to my creative agency team at Prime Concepts Group, Inc. (PrimeConcepts.com), who've sat through many meetings where I drew my countless mind maps, illustrations, and training concepts. A special mention to Barry Owens and Tiffany Sowa, who were instrumental in the rewrite of the original manuscript. And to Devan Horning who set deadlines, guided me, and kept me accountable to get this released to the world. As the CEO and leader of such a creative and innovative team, I want to thank you for all your talents and abilities. You've helped me refine these concepts and practice them in our personal and professional lives. It's in this living laboratory where many of these concepts were refined. Your diverse nature, unique personality styles, generational differences, and educational experience have given the unique insights for delivering the concepts in this book. My gratitude also goes out to all my clients, audience members, podcast listeners, blog readers, and social media tribe members.

I have realized that *the more I learn, the less I really know.* What I mean by that is, at this stage of my life, I've finally figured out that there's always more to learn and that practice doesn't make perfection, practice makes improvement. The scariest individuals I know think they know everything but haven't yet figured out what they don't know. I know that may sound confusing, but those people who think they know it all are closed off from new ideas and new opportunities. I know that's not you, or you wouldn't have picked up this book.

And when you think about it, isn't that what superpower is all about? How we can do more with less, how we can make decisions faster and better, and how we can navigate the new diverse landscape of the modern world to produce the results we want in business, leadership, and life.

PART 1:
RETHINK

CHAPTER ONE:
THE BIRTH OF A SUPERHERO

The kid with the pistol had a problem to solve. He needed answers. His life sucked, but he had a plan. The guy on the other side of the counter didn't seem to care and wouldn't listen. How could he make him listen?

"Bob, please," the kid said. He'd read the name on the guy's shirt. People who wear name tags should be better at customer service. Bob was a big guy in a small apron. His only job was to be nice and stock shelves and help customers. Why wasn't he helping?

It was probably the gun, the kid thought. It was in his back pocket. He hadn't pulled it on the guy, wasn't even thinking of pulling it on him, had never pulled it on anyone. But he looked like the kind of punk that would. He made sure of that. Wild hair, army jacket, hard face. "Don't mess with me" was the look. It was a disguise.

Inside, the kid was scared most of the time. Not sure of his value, unaware of his abilities. Afraid of the world and himself, of what he might do next. He'd done some dumb stuff — real dumb — and had been bounced out of school, run out of foster families, put out on the street, and now rented a rathole place of his own in the housing projects. He'd done some time in a juvenile detention center. He was only 15 years old and doing a hard stretch on the outside now — maybe life. But he could do better. He knew it. He had something inside him. He had a plan that would change his trajectory. His life would be better, he would be happier, the world would finally make sense if only Bob would just friggin' help him for a second.

"Come on, man," the kid said. "Tell me what I need to do."

You've picked up this book because you are in search of some answers, too. Maybe you want to be a better leader, or do better business, or live better. I am here to show you how you can make all those goals happen if you put in the work. You won't have to beg me for the information. You won't need a gun. *You have superpowers.*

Go ahead. Roll your eyes. "Superpowers! Like Superman? This guy's full of it." I know that's what you're thinking. I might have thought that, too, long ago. But that wasn't working out for me, being closed-minded, not believing in myself, and blaming others for my troubles. It was time to raise my expectations for myself.

I was that kid at the store counter back in 1974. I was in trouble, but good trouble. I had just gotten my first lead on a potential customer for my brand-new business. Exciting times, right? But I had no idea how to deliver the service I was selling. I'd put out some fliers and business cards, promoting myself as a house painter (and offering light construction). The only walls I had ever painted were inside the Hennepin County Juvenile Detention Center, a punishment for swearing. I painted an entire @#&!ing wing of the place. As for construction, I had zero experience. That's why the cards read "light construction." So, yeah. I was in way over my head. I had to meet the potential client in about an hour to discuss the job, make an estimate and create a proposal. I'd rushed to the local

CHAPTER ONE: THE BIRTH OF A SUPERHERO

paint store in a desperate attempt to get some information, any clue that could help me pull off the transformation.

"What do I do?" I asked Bob for like the tenth time. "I'm serious."

It wasn't that the guy was bad at his job, but I was bad at asking for help. I looked like a troublemaker out to give him a bad time (Dennis the Menace gone juvenile delinquent), not a serious customer in serious trouble. Anyway, what could he tell a kid about running a painting business?

Bob took a deep breath like he was gathering a sigh and finally answered on the exhale.

"Follow me," he said.

I followed him over to the paint aisle, where he silently pried the lid off the top of a paint can. Then he grabbed a brush from the shelf and dipped it into the bucket. He waved me over. Closer. Right there, his hand said. Then he flicked the brush at me, splattering my clothes and shoes.

"What the hell are you doing?" I said.

Bob turned back to the shelf.

"You didn't look like a painter," he said, pressing the lid back down on the paint can. "Now you do."

WHAT'S YOUR ORIGIN STORY?

That's how it all started for me. That was the moment of transformation or at least when I first put on the paint-spattered costume. I still had to see the potential client and convince them that I was the real deal. I needed to fool myself first.

We were all superheroes when we were small. Did you have a cape and a costume? Did you play the part of Superman, Wonder Woman, Batman, Spiderman, or one of the other heroes who swooped in, thwarted the bad guys, and solved all the world's problems? As kids, we believe in magic, and we have faith that these special skills are real and not just for comic books and cartoons. We believe that we really do have superpowers and, in our childlike minds, have confidence that we can conquer the world.

What happened along the way? Who squashed our beliefs in our own superpowers? Whoever it was (and watch out, it just might have been someone who shows up in the mirror every morning), they forgot how important hero narratives are to human success and achievement. We need to be able to reinvent ourselves as superheroes. It's part of how we're wired as human beings, and we've been doing it for thousands of years. I don't care if your role model was Batman, the Black Panther, or Beowulf. I'm here to tell you that you were on the right track. Regardless of how old you are, where you are in your career, how long you've been in business, it's not too late for you to join the ranks of the superhero you loved most, take your power back, and truly conquer your world... in business, leadership, and life.

Are you ready to take the first step?

FEEL YOUR SUPERPOWERS

Take a moment. Find a quiet place. Then close your eyes and see yourself as a superhero. What is your name? What are you wearing? What color is your cape? Do you have a mask? Is there an emblem on your chest? Do you have a magic weapon of some kind, like a sword that starts glowing when the bad guys are approaching from far off? What type of superpowers do you possess? What is your leadership style? Are you a "Wizard of Innovation," "Marketing Magician," or "Number Ninja"?

Whatever these amazing superpowers are, we're going to take a look at how you can begin to expand, unlock, develop, and use them in your daily life.

It may sound silly to think of yourself as a superhero, but it is the first and most important step in unlocking your power.

CHAPTER ONE: THE BIRTH OF A SUPERHERO

You must start to see, think, and act differently than you may have in the past. The only constant in life is change. And change is a choice. Choose to get happy about change. If you're not changing, adapting, and growing, it will be a challenge to work in different ways to get better results.

Let your superhero self out to play.

THE STARTING POINT OF YOUR JOURNEY

Where are you in your life right now? How would you rate yourself on your personal and professional success? How did the pandemic of 2020 and beyond impact you? It shook me to the core. Friends and family died. Many of my colleagues lost their businesses due to the shutdowns, and for many, morale was at an all-time low. While there are always outside influences beyond our control, what we can control is our mindset, attitude, and actions. As my good friend, W. Mitchell, says, "It's not what happens to you that matters; it's what you do about it."

Over the years, I've had the privilege of working with many millionaires and even a few billionaires. You would think that people who earn a lot of money would feel successful across the board. Many are not. They are driven to achieve more, to acquire more, to have more, and to do more, but are unfulfilled in other areas of life.

This morning I started reading a book written by one of my clients, Jean Palmer Heck. The book is *Tough Talks for Tough Times*, a must-read for anybody in management or leadership. She shared an illustration and concept about a campaign that Toyota implemented a few years back called "GAME ON." It stands for Gain Advantage, Monetize Everything, Overlook Nothing. That's one of my favorite acronyms because it showed an entire organization how to harness its untapped superpowers.

In her book, Jean told how Toyota Motor Company launched that initiative throughout the company with the twin goals of reducing fixed costs and increasing top-line revenues. It saved Toyota more than $235 million. I'm referencing it because it's a great strategy that can apply to our own lives. I have a few adaptations.

GAIN ADVANTAGE

What are you doing to leverage your talents and expertise? Who is in your inner circle and why? What other resources are in your success library? Who are your mentors? Are you surrounded by critical thinkers that will call you out if you're whining, complaining or expressing victimhood? There is no such thing as job security — the pandemic proved that — what you can rely on is skills security. If you want to gain an advantage, you need to improve your skill sets continuously.

MONETIZE EVERYTHING

How are you maximizing your efforts, managing your money, and creating wealth? Are you finding yourself distracted by Facebook, TikTok, Instagram, or spending too much time binge-watching Netflix? Do you have savings, investments, and real estate? Is your money working for you? Is the majority of your day spent on the highest and best use of your time?

OVERLOOK NOTHING

Are you willing to dig deep and take a good look at all of the areas of your life? Think about your health and fitness, security and wealth, prosperity consciousness, spirituality, family, social life and relationships, mental development, daily habits and routines, life purpose, and contribution as they relate to your personal and professional life. Just like any trip or journey that you're going to take, you need to know first where you are now, understand where you want to go, and then figure out how you're going to get there. This may sound simple, but that doesn't mean that it's easy.

WHERE'S MY SUPER SUIT?

It's time to look more closely at what has led you to this moment.

Life has a way of giving us challenges and unforeseen obstacles that create roadblocks on our path to fulfillment and success. How you deal with those obstacles and challenges creates learning experiences that develop your character and personality. Every obstacle you have ever faced, and every response you ever made to those obstacles, directed your path and shaped your superhero.

To make that journey, though, you need to know your starting point. That means taking an assessment of where you are now. We will start this process by performing a personal assessment and capturing your thoughts and ideas.

As an action step, download the *Hero Handbook* at ProfitRichResults.com/hero-handbook. The first step in the superpower process is to get a benchmark of where you are in many areas of your life. The *Hero Handbook* has useful metrics and is a companion guide to this book and to help you make the most of your journey.

Set aside time on your schedule to write down your perception of where you are in your life right now. This can be an amazing experience if you're honest with yourself and fully immerse yourself in the process. Yes, of course, there's our perspective of ourselves, and there are other people's perspectives of us. For now, I just want you to get your own perspective down on paper.

There are no right or wrong answers. This is not a test. You don't have to share it with anyone. Let go of shame, guilt, and ego. This is an exercise that I suggest you do at least twice a year. It will help you track and accelerate your growth process.

Download and print your *Hero Handbook* and write answers to the questions and action steps at the end of each chapter. Superpowerbook.com/downloads

CHAPTER 1 KEY CONCEPTS:

- What is your origin story?
- Who's in your inner circle?
- Are you maximizing your talents, time, and expertise?
- Where are you in your life right now?

ACTION STEPS:

Write answers to the following questions:

HEALTH AND FITNESS

1. How much do you weigh?

2. How much do you think you should weigh?

3. During a typical week, how many days do you engage in vigorous physical activity for at least 20 minutes?

4. During a typical week, how many days do you engage in mild physical activity for at least 30 minutes at a time? How much do you think you should weigh?

5. What is your favorite cardio activity?

6. What is your favorite strength-training activity?

7. Do you know your resting heart rate? If so, what is it?

8. On a typical day, how many hours do you spend on screen time? Categorize it by your phone, tablet, television, playing video games, or using a computer? How much of it is business vs personal? How much is productive vs distraction?

9. On a typical day, how many alcoholic drinks, including beer and wine, do you drink?

10. On a typical day, how many soft drinks do you consume?

11. On a scale of 1 to 10, how often do you feel stressed, with 1 being not very much and 10 being daily?

12. Are you taking any medications?

13. Do you take vitamins?

14. On a typical night, how many hours do you sleep?

15. On a scale of 1 to 10, how would you rate your health and fitness, with 1 being poor and 10 being excellent?

CAREER

1. Do you work for someone else, or are you self-employed?

2. What is your position title?

3. What are the top three skill sets required for success in your position?

4. How would you rate yourself on the performance of those skill sets (1 to 10, with 1 being poor and 10 being excellent)?

5. How do you describe to your friends and family what you do?

6. Are you an executive, manager, or staff person?

7. Do you manage other people?

8. How many different companies have you worked for?

9. Is your career mentally stimulating or boring?

10. What are three reasons you love your current career/business?

11. What are three elements you wish you could change about your career/business?

12. Are you getting paid what you're worth?

13. What are you doing to keep your skill sets current each year?

14. Describe your ideal dream job.

WEALTH AND FINANCIAL SECURITY

1. Do you use a program like Quicken® to track and manage your finances?

2. How much money do you earn each year?

3. How much money do you save each year?

4. How much money do you invest each year?

5. How much much debt do you have?

6. Amount of short-term debt (credit cards, loans, etc.)?

7. Amount of long-term debt (mortgage, business loans, etc.)?

8. Your total assets?

9. Your total liabilities?

CHAPTER ONE: THE BIRTH OF A SUPERHERO

10. Do you have a retirement plan, a 401(k) or IRA?

11. Do you have health and life insurance?

12. Do you live on a budget, or do you make your financial decisions without any budget?

RELATIONSHIPS

1. Who are your top five friends that you spend the most time with and why?

2. Who is your best friend? Why?

3. Are you in an intimate relationship?

4. Rate those relationships on scale of 1 to 10, with 1 being poor and 10 being outstanding.

5. Are you single, married, or divorced? (circle one)

6. Are you a parent?

7. How social do you consider yourself to be (on a scale of 1 to 10)?

SPIRITUALITY

1. Do you believe in a higher power?

2. Do you consider yourself spiritual or religious?

3. Do you follow any spiritual path or practice (e.g., meditation, yoga, chanting)?

4. What have been your most important experiences, if any, concerning your relationship with God (fill in the blank for what you identify as God) or your higher power?

5. What do you believe in that gives meaning to your life?

6. What would you say is your purpose in life?

CHAPTER ONE: THE BIRTH OF A SUPERHERO

IDENTIFY YOUR STRENGTHS, UNDERSTAND YOURSELF AND OTHERS

For additional insights into your personality and way of thinking, you may want to explore the professional assessments from **ProfitRichResults.com**

I suggest these top three to start:

Self-Assessment - Create productive relationships in personal and professional life with the DISC® Self-Assessment

ProfitRichResults.com/product/self-assessment

- Learn to foster productive relationships in your personal and professional life
- Understand what drives others around you
- Get your personalized, comprehensive report emailed directly to you

Sales-Assessment - Improve your sales by improving yourself with an individual DISC® Sales Assessmen

ProfitRichResults.com/product/sales-assessment

- Improve your sales approach by learning to apply your strengths
- Learn to adapt to different buying styles and maximize your sales
- Get your personalized, comprehensive report emailed directly to you

Leadership Assessment - Lead your team to success with DISC® Leadership Assessment

21

ProfitRichResults.com/product/leadership-assessment

- Improve your own method of communication with all your employees
- Learn to hire effectively for your company and management style
- Get your personalized, comprehensive report emailed directly to you

These tools can help you identify your strengths and weaknesses while outlining a road map for improvement.

CHAPTER TWO:
CREATING THE SUPERHERO MINDSET

WHAT YOU BELIEVE about yourself, your world, and the way you think has a powerful effect on what you can achieve. Do you see yourself as a creative and innovative thinker? Do you like yourself? Are you proud of what you have accomplished in your life so far? Do you have a can-do attitude? Or do your belief systems — your B.S. — create roadblocks and limitations that prevent you from accessing your superpowers?

I was at a business conference a while ago, and one of the presenters was Bonnie McElveen-Hunter. She was an ambassador for the United States to Finland. She is also president and CEO of Pace Communications and the American Red Cross chairperson. Talk about a superhero! This amazing woman continues to use her superpowers for business success and to impact the planet positively. When asked what has helped her become the superwoman she is today, she said, "When I was a child, my mother made me write the words 'I can't' on a piece of paper, put it in a shoebox, and bury it in the backyard. The words 'I can't' have never been a part of my vocabulary. My only option is 'I can.' I just have to figure out a way to make it happen."

"I CAN"

Have you ever wanted to try a different approach but found that you just weren't sure how, or even if, you could do it? I think we all feel that way sometimes. What holds us back from taking action? Is it our belief system, our programming, or our conditioning? Is it a combination of all three?

We're talking about the transition from "I can't" to "I can." For a superhero (and for a successful entrepreneur), a positive mindset is foundational for success.

I've been an entrepreneur since I was 12 years old when I started my car-washing business. All I needed was the hose, a bucket, some dish soap, and some dirty cars. The summers were hot, and the winters were freezing in Minneapolis, Minnesota, so this was definitely a seasonal business. I was in sixth grade, and I washed cars after school. I was fascinated by how easy it was to make money. Of course, for a 12-year-old, even $20 seems like a lot of money, or at least it did back in the 1970s. I was adopted into a single-parent home, bounced around foster homes, and spent much of my time on my own running around the streets.

At 15 years old, I found myself living in the government housing projects in North Minneapolis, paying $17 a month for rent. Don't get me wrong. I didn't miss any meals, and, yes, I know that many people had a much more traumatic childhood than I did. Stick with me. This is not a sob story.

At the time, I was considered an at-risk youth, a teenager who seemed unlikely to complete school or transition successfully into adulthood and achieve economic self-sufficiency. My junior and senior high schools had alternative programs for at-risk kids where work experience would be counted as educational credits towards graduating. This meant I had to attend school for only one hour a day in the morning and then go to work for at least six hours. My employer was required to submit an employment report weekly, and it counted as credit for my grade.

Here's where it gets really cool. I realized that if I was my own boss, I could fill out my own employment report, and I'd have control over my life. (I'm sharing this with you so you can get a sense of my "I can" thought processes back then — and today.)

At 15 years old, I was trying to figure out how to make money in different ways than everybody else in my economically challenged neighborhood. I remember sitting down with the phone book (this was before the internet), looking at all the business listings and trying to decide which type I could run. I knew it had to be a job that didn't take much money to get started.

Then I came across "painting."

That was it. I would start a painting company and become an entrepreneur. Why painting? Because, as I mentioned earlier, I had a little bit of experience painting from dropping F-bombs in the detention center. I painted a LOT of walls.

I went to my friend, Steve Sims, for a logo, business cards, and flyers. Being resourceful, we printed all the advertising during shop class. The flyers read, "Saeks Painting and Light Construction." I added "light construction" as a way to make it easier to get jobs. It was "light" construction because I had zero construction experience.

I didn't have any customers, equipment, or experience, but I thought I was in business because I had cards and flyers. I put them everywhere. On car windshields in parking lots, and on grocery store bulletin boards. I went door-to-door and inserted them in mailboxes. NOTE: Don't do that. It's illegal.

I had a job at the time as a cashier making minimum wage at the Army-Navy Surplus Store on Fourth Street and Hennepin Avenue in downtown Minneapolis. Each night after work, I checked my answering machine to see if it had any lead calls from my grassroots marketing efforts.

One night, finally, the answering machine light was blinking. I was so excited. My first lead! My excitement soon turned to fear and anxiety as I realized that I didn't have a clue what I was doing.

My negative self-talk kicked in. "You can't do that. You don't have parents, you're not smart enough, you're not old enough, you don't have enough experience, you don't have any money, you don't know how to prepare a proposal for a painting job. What are you thinking?" Now at the time, I didn't know what self-talk was. I just heard that little voice in my head trying to hold me back. I had a spark of inspiration, but my negative self-talk was trying to extinguish the flame.

Sound familiar? How many times in your life have you been faced with an opportunity, only to let the little voice in your head hold you back or talk you out of taking action?

SEEKING OUT EXPERTS

I knew I needed help from an expert. That's when I met Bob at Bryant Avenue Painting. After he splattered me with paint so that I would look the part, he outfitted me with all the tools I would need.

He gave me a painter's cap, a calculator, and instructions on how to measure the rooms. Then, God bless him, he sent me on my way to the prospect's house.

The prospect lived in an older two-story home, with a nicely groomed lawn in the south part of Minneapolis. Now I had two voices in my head. One voice told me to go for it and one said I was F*@king crazy. Thank goodness, I listened to the positive voice and knocked on the door.

A nice man in his 50s opened the door and smiled.

"Hi, I'm Roger," he said.

I shook his hand.

"I'm Ford, and I'm here to gather the details for your painting project so I can prepare the proposal."

Roger walked me from room to room, explaining what he wanted. In the kitchen, he wanted the walls painted with KILZ and the windows glazed. In the hallways, he wanted semigloss paint. In the bedrooms, he wanted flat paint. In the bathroom, he wanted gloss paint. Then he pointed at the ceilings where they were cracked around the ceiling fans and said he wanted me to fix the ceilings and paint them. Now, I was in literally way over my head.

I didn't know what KILZ meant or what glazing windows meant. I thought paint was paint. I didn't know flat from semigloss or oil-based from water-based paint.

I was overwhelmed and wondering if I should continue or just make a break for it. I put on my best fake smile to hide my fear, took a lot of notes, and measured the rooms. I explained to Roger that I would need to go back to my office to prepare the proposal and that I would be back in about an hour.

My office. Ha. I didn't even have a paintbrush. Back at the store, Bob helped me calculate all of the painting supplies, equipment, and labor that I would need to complete the job. He gave me suggestions on how much to charge and how to prepare the proposal. I was so grateful for his expertise. He gave me suggestions on how much to charge and how to prepare the proposal. I was so grateful for his expertise.

I headed back to Roger's house. This time when the door opened, his wife was with him. She took one look at me and stepped behind her husband.

"This isn't going to go well," I thought.

I handed them the proposal with shaky hands. My heart was pounding.

"The price for this job is $1,025," I said. "I'll need 50 percent upfront as a deposit, with 50 percent due on completion."

Roger's wife looked at me, then at the quote, and then back at me.

"Do you have any experience?" she said.

This was a critical point in my new business. Do I explain to this nice couple that my only experience was painting the entire north wing of the Hennepin County Detention Center? No Way!

"I'll offer you a money-back guarantee," I heard myself saying, surprised at how quick it came to me. "If you're not 100-percent satisfied with the results, I'll give you a full refund. No questions asked."

Then I held my breath.

"Honey," Roger's wife said. "Write him a check."

He did.

I sat in my car — which, by the way, had no insurance, tags, or title (you can probably guess why) — looking at that check for a long time. It was more money than I could earn working at the army surplus store in three months. The $525 deposit money was enough to buy initial supplies and start-up equipment. But I would need help to complete the job.

It was the end of October, and the weather was already starting to turn cold. I went back to Bryant Avenue Paint and stood outside in the sleeting rain. I needed a crew and asked every person walking inside if they were looking for more painting work. Finally, after three hours, I found my guys. My offer was to pay them 60 percent and I'd keep 40 percent.

Many painters, at least the ones I hired, liked to do two things — paint and drink. They didn't want to market, prospect, or sell. Lucky for them those were my superpowers.

By the end of my first year in my business, when I was 16, I had three painting crews working for me, and their average age was 40. I earned more than $35,000 that first year. Not bad for a kid from the projects in the late 1970s. In today's economy, that amount would equate to more than $250,000.

Do you know what happens when a kid from the projects gets $35,000? He spends $36,000. It took me a few years to fully understand business operations, accounting, and inventory control. And then there were other skills to pick up, like leading successful teams, direct response marketing, generating leads, and closing new and repeat sales. But I did.

All this was a long time ago. I had a chip on my shoulder for growing up without any parental guidance or much formal education for many years. That chip splintered away over time as I read books, listened to audio programs, attended seminars, and made better distinctions in my life. My point is that you and your staff can improve your performance and results, regardless of your circumstances or level of success. You can turn off the "I can't" voice and listen to the "I can" voice anytime you choose.

MAKING SUPERPOWER CHOICES

That is the foundational element of this book. The difference between your superhero and where you are right now can be measured by the choices you make, right now, about what you believe you can and can't do. It's about rethinking, reframing, and rebooting your mindset. It's about reigniting your passion for personal and professional growth.

I'm sharing my experiences and insights here not to convince you about how wonderful I am — believe me, there is always someone richer, healthier, and more successful — but to help you get traction when it comes to thinking, acting, and performing.

CHAPTER TWO: CREATING THE SUPERHERO MINDSET

CHAPTER 2 KEY CONCEPTS:

- What is holding you back from taking massive action?
- Who's in your corner? Who is your expert?
- What choices can you make now to reboot your mindset?

ACTION STEPS:

Here are five action steps you can take right now to shift your mindset for Superpower Success.

1. Write in the Hero Handbook or journal at least a few times each week, if not daily, to record your feelings and monitor your progress.

2. Put yourself first on your list of priorities. If you don't take care of yourself, you won't have the energy to take care of anyone else.

3. Recognize that your thoughts determine your beliefs, your beliefs determine your behaviors, your behaviors determine your habits and actions, and your habits and actions lead to your results. If you want better results, then you need to make sure that your beliefs, behaviors, habits, and actions are in alignment with your goals.

4. Shift from saying, *"I have to…"* to *"I get to…"* This is a choice, and how you frame it subconsciously and verbally has a big impact on your actions and results.

5. Take personal accountability for your life. You can't change the past, but you can change your perspective. More about that in future chapters. For now, focus on today and celebrate small victories each night as you put your head on your pillow.

CHAPTER THREE:
THE SUPERPOWER OF PROSPERITY CONSCIOUSNESS

RICK WASN'T BUYING it. I could tell. He was my last call of the day. The director of operations for a wholesale drug distributor, a business I didn't know much about at the time. All I knew was that FoxMeyer Drug Company had carpets, lots of them, and I saw dollar signs. I was 26 years old and on business number three: Saeks Carpet Cleaning Company. I had three crews steaming for me around the country. I was the rainmaker, responsible for bringing in every drop of new business.

I'd come a long way since my early paint-spattered days. I'd learned how to find, attract and keep customers. I'd learned how to believe in myself, win contracts, take care of the customer, and get the job done. Most importantly, I'd tapped into a prosperity mindset. You may have heard of this. It was popularized in the mainstream a few years back when it was the subject of *The Secret*, a book and movie.

So, what's the secret? In a nutshell, it's about the positive, magnetic energy we create when we focus on our goals — any goal. What we focus on in the universe, we attract. Supper, sex, success. You can manifest positive results in your personal and professional life by harnessing and applying positive mental energy at every opportunity. It's definitely a superpower. It starts with believing in yourself, that you are worthy and deserving and the world is rich with resources and ripe with opportunity. There is enough business out there for you to compete. There are plenty of fish in the sea. You can attract love. You can attract happiness. You can be healthy and wealthy if you apply for the job. But you have to apply. You have to believe.

If that all sounds like a bunch of New Age nonsense to you, consider the alternative. Life is a random series of events where nothing works out for you, you have no chance, you shouldn't even try, so you don't. Only the lucky thrive and they did less to deserve their good fortune. What's worse, you think being positive is for suckers and flim-flam men trying to sell you on self-improvement. That would be a sorry way to go through life.

I don't care if people think that I look like a sucker picking up self-help books, trying fad diets, and pasting up dream boards. I'm a happy fool and a successful one. Why? Because the energy I put into every hope and desire I have in my life creates a better quality of life. Even when I fail or they are not the results I set out to achieve, they are always learning experiences that make me stronger. I live better today because I tried yesterday.

Case in point, Rick at FoxMeyer Drug Company. He seemed like a "No" at first. But I kept at him. He leaned deep into his office chair, elbow on the armrest, propping his head up with one hand. He had one finger curled across his lips. Was he trying to look thoughtful, or was he shushing me? Didn't matter. I kept talking. I knew how to play this or thought that

CHAPTER THREE: THE SUPERPOWER OF PROSPERITY CONSCIOUSNESS

I did. I didn't push myself or my services. I pushed the benefits of clean carpets.

"They'll make a better impression," I said. "They'll reduce your maintenance costs," I said. I kept going and going until Rick finally seemed to hear enough. He lifted his finger from his face and pointed it at me.

"Tell me," Rick said. "What do you know about computers?"

Now, raise your hand if you saw that question coming. I didn't. It was 1984. Who in the world besides Bill Gates and Steve Jobs was thinking about computers? And what did that have to do with cleaning Rick's carpets? But I played along because I knew what a computer was. It was a keyboard you plugged into a television. Hardly sophisticated — no hard drives or graphic capabilities — the machines were simple by today's standards. They were good for playing primitive games or writing basic reports.

"I know a little," I said. That much was true. I'd always been fascinated with technology and had messed around with a few of the early models like the Commodore 64 and Amiga systems. But if he was talking about mainframe computers, the kind that took up entire rooms and was operated by men in lab coats, well, that would be a different story. But at least he was talking, so I said yes just to see where he was going.

Where he was going would change my life in ways that are still reverberating to this day.

And THAT's the superpower of positive thinking, of the prosperity mindset. I was about to unlock an opportunity that never would have presented itself to me had I not been all about the "Yes, I can." Like Henry Ford said, "There are two types of people in the world. Those who think they can, and those who think they can't. They are both right."

37

I THINK I CAN

Here's what is incredible about that moment in Rick's office. I didn't recognize it for what it was — life-changing. I was focused on getting the sale and just humoring the guy with his computer questions. But one thing led to another, and another, and suddenly it's 30 years later and here I am writing furiously, trying to remember every detail of how this domino fell. I want to get down for you the exact steps you can take to attract and capture opportunities to enjoy greater success like I have since I said yes in Rick's office. It was only another stop in my journey, but a crucial one toward understanding who I was and what I wanted out of life — and what I did not want. Look, it's a long story and we'll get to all of it. The point is that I got the carpet cleaning contract for 65 locations. The second point is that I walked out of Rick's office with a job. I said yes to his question, to computers, to the universe. He hired me on the spot. I haven't been the same since.

Here's what happened.

FoxMeyer Drug Company was ahead of the times. They were distributing drugs throughout the Kmart Pharmacy chain of 2000 stores, and they were implementing computer systems at each location to manage inventory. They needed trainers that could travel to each location, install the new computers and software, and train the pharmacy staff how to use them. They needed a guy like me, is how Rick put it.

He said he liked my determination. It came through in my can-do attitude, how I communicated, in my salesmanship and customer service skills. I'd won him over and got him thinking about possibilities. He could see that what I didn't know about computers I could learn. I had all the other skills he was looking for in the position.

(Detour: A lesson that I carry through in my future businesses is to hire for attitude and train for skills. If you just hire someone with the skills without the proper attitude, they can contaminate the culture in your organization.)

Fine, Ford. But why take the job? You had one. Maybe the best one. You were a business owner, master of your fate, in charge of your days, lifestyle, success. No one to answer to but yourself. No one to tell you what to do. Why would you want a boss? These are questions you might be asking yourself right now. They're questions maybe I should have asked myself at the time.

Listen: Some of us learn the hard way, but at least we are willing to learn. That's one lesson here. And it's why I took the job. I'm an explorer, an adventurer. I live to climb the next mountain. Worst case scenario, I fall off the mountain I have a story to tell on the way down. Best case, I have some fun, make some money and learn. Either way, the general manager could run my carpet cleaning business until I returned. I had nothing to lose.

For the next three years, I traveled across the country, helping hundreds of Kmart pharmacists learn how to use computers. I got pretty good at the job. All of that early technology is obsolete today, but what I learned about myself in the process continues to be valuable. I was popular around the drug counters for taking complicated subjects and breaking them down to make them easy to understand and implement. In the industry's parlance, I was interfacing between the software developers and end-users. All that means in real talk is that I was helping people leverage digital tools.

I still do. Not for FoxMeyer Drug Company, but for my own clients at Prime Concepts Group and audiences around the globe. We don't clean carpets, but we can help with just about any other challenge businesses face today, digital, strategic, or otherwise. But that's a story for later. It's not even the moral of this one.

WHAT HAVE I DONE?

So, there I was going from town-to-town transferring knowledge at Kmarts and rising in the ranks at the corporate office. Climbing the ladder. Bigger offices, better titles, more pay, more responsibilities. All good, right? Could have been my whole life. But then I met Luther. He was the man I was to replace as the director of purchasing. I'd just been promoted. Again. And, boy, was Luther not happy for me.

Here is what he said when I came to his office for training.

"I'll be damned if I'm going to train you to take over my position," he said. "Come back in three months. You can take over on my last day."

So that's what I did. Forget the training. I'd figure it out on the job like I always did.

Late on a Friday three months later I walked into Luther's office just like he asked. The old guy had been at the company for more than half of his life. He had put 35 years of blood, sweat, and tears into FoxMeyer Drug Company, and the day he turned 65, they just asked him to leave. Mandatory retirement. I was there when he put his pencil down at 5 p.m. Then he picked up his overcoat, put on his hat, and walked out. No going-away party, no goodbyes, no special celebration. Luther just gathered his few belongings and left. I barely remember what he looked like. When the door closed, it was as if he had never been there at all. It never happened. He never mattered, not there anyway.

I am eternally grateful to the old guy, though. Luther didn't want to, but he taught me a lesson. I quit the next day.

CHAPTER THREE: THE SUPERPOWER OF PROSPERITY CONSCIOUSNESS

THE BIRTH OF AN INVENTION

Three years. Three stinking years I spent learning that lesson. Feel like maybe it shouldn't have taken so long to learn that I wanted more out of life than just a job. I'm an entrepreneur. That's what I find rewarding. That's what gets me up in the morning. Even if I was good at a job, even if I loved it, it never would love me back. Oh well. At least now, I didn't have one. What to do next? I still had a decent income from my carpet cleaning business but couldn't see myself cleaning carpets for the rest of my life either. Maybe a girlfriend? She would keep me company, perhaps even love me. That's the way it works. But there was no way I was attracting a romantic partner (even with my prosperity mindset) until I cleaned myself up a little and my apartment a lot. I was doing that a day after I left the drug company when another domino fell.

You don't know this about me yet because it's not that important to the story and you wouldn't believe it anyway if you saw me today, but I was once graceful. And fast as hell on skates. In my youth, I was a speed skater, good enough to be an Olympic hopeful. Hey, I'm from Minnesota. That's what we do up there. Or what I used to do, anyway. By age 30, I'd let go of that dream to focus on my business goals. But I still loved the wind in my face and the ground rushing beneath my feet. So, I cycled. Cycling uses the same muscle groups as skating. It came naturally to me. I still enjoy it today. The difference now is, I have a two-car garage for all my bikes and gear. Back then, I had them all piled up in my two-bedroom apartment. Not sexy.

Or could they be? That's where this story gets interesting. I was looking for a way to display my bicycles, high-priced Italian models, real works of art. They should be hanging on the wall, I thought. They have appeal, and that would solve my clutter problem. But how? A hook wouldn't do. I'd damage the ceiling and lose my deposit.

But what about …?

Hear that? That's the start of an idea forming. A $50 million dollar idea.

Write this down. When you focus on a problem with a prosperity mindset, your mind works to help you solve it. Your mind is your friend. It wants to help. Let it. Don't focus on negativity. *This won't work because of that. That's dumb. It's all been done.* Focus on a challenge and look for positive solutions. *This could work because ... I like this idea ... now we're getting somewhere!* Cheer your little buddy brain on. Keep going. Don't censor yourself. There are no bad ideas. You'll hit one out of the park if you really believe it could be the next one and just keep swinging. This is more than an exercise. This is a superpower.

I didn't know any of that at the time, just like I didn't know much about computers a few years before. But I said, "Yes. I can do this." Ten minutes later, I was a millionaire.

Okay. No one came to my door and handed me a check. I had to see my idea through and get it to market. That was a painstaking process full of many false starts and failings. It would be years before my company grew to more than 100 employees and generated over $50 million in sales.

But I was on my way.

I THINK I CAN'T

I invented a pole, basically. It was a tough sell in the beginning. I mean, it was a stick with some hooks on it. But it was a quality stick. Nice hooks. Made of oak. Real handsome. Fit floor-to-ceiling, adjustable to any height. An elegant solution for hanging a fine bicycle in your living room. Was there a market for it beyond me? Didn't seem like it from the people I showed it to.

That was demoralizing. And a lesson. Be careful who you let into your life, influence your ideas, step on your dreams. Negativity is viral and nasty. Like a bug spray, it kills dreams

CHAPTER THREE: THE SUPERPOWER OF PROSPERITY CONSCIOUSNESS

dead. I've seen it destroy teams in the workplace. I've seen it destroy people in their personal lives. It's nearly destroyed me a time or two. I'm sure we've all had our run-ins. The worst is when we do it to ourselves with negative self-talk.

Here is what the voices in my head were telling me at the time. "You idiot, why would you just leave a job with a great salary and benefits? You think that stick in your hand is going to solve your problems, pay for your insurance? You think it will sell? Get real. Get a job. Get help, man. You don't know what you are doing."

The voice was partly right. I really didn't know what I was doing. But here's what I had going for me: I'm stubborn. I won't always admit I'm wrong, even to myself about myself. I wasn't about to prove me right. So, I turned my negative energy into positive action. At least that is what I told my better self as I pressed on. But just in case I was wrong about being right, I decided to get some help.

I believe in experts. I reached out for input on my idea from a couple of business consultants. Each of them told me that I should forget it. It would only sell in the short term, they said. It was too expensive ($189 retail). The competition was a 99-cent metal hook. They said I would saturate the market within three years and then be out of business.

Those guys sucked. I sucked. It all sucked. That's the sinkhole I found myself in every morning. But every morning I kept climbing out and looking for another way to prove myself. Right or wrong, it didn't matter. I was out to prove my worth to somebody.

I bet you can relate. I know there've been times in your life when you had to make a tough decision and your self-talk convinced you either into it or out of it. In my heart of hearts, I knew I'd made the right decision. I just didn't know exactly what I was going to do next. It was now almost six months into this new business venture, and I had depleted all my savings. I was living on fumes and credit cards. There had to be a better way. I knew there were people who would purchase the bike rack if I could just get the right combination of marketing message, target market, and marketing method. Unlike at the paint store or Rick's office, the bike racks were not going the direction I wanted them to when I just kept pushing.

Maybe that was the problem. I needed to start pulling.

Up to this point, I'd had a tiny bit of luck getting a few local bicycle shops to carry my product on consignment. That didn't do much for my cash flow, but it helped a little. I went back to them and this time, instead of pushing my rack on them, I interviewed them. I pulled. I wanted to know where they purchased their products, how they made their buying decisions, what trade shows they went to, what magazines they read, and which vendors they purchased from and why.

Then I called those vendors and interviewed them to determine their channels of distribution, which trade shows they went to, and how they manufactured, marketed, and sold their products. Finally, the clues I needed to transform my fledgling small business were coming into focus. Now I was getting somewhere! Trouble is, I had just discovered that where I was, was nowhere near the place I needed to be. Where I needed to be, where it all was happening in the industry, was in California. In three weeks. That's when and where Interbike, the largest bicycle trade show in the United States, was happening. I had to get my sticks together and be there.

So, look. I knew I had a product with sales potential. I knew it was more than a stick. I was just being self-deprecating earlier when I called it a pole, showing you how negative self-talk infected my mindset and held me back at first. The truth is, I was proud of the idea and the prototype. I'd sketched up the plans and had a local woodshop put it together for me. It was a solid oak bicycle storage rack with interlocking pieces that enabled it to adjust to different ceiling heights with furniture levelers at the bottom to adjust the tension to keep it in place manually. Just like I drew it up. It worked beautifully in my apartment. I knew I wasn't the only person storing bikes in a limited space. I knew all of the other bicycle racers had at least two or three bicycles. Then there were the kids in college dorms, apartment dwellers, and the people living with bikes in limited spaces around the globe. I realized I had identified a problem and an opportunity. But the way I was going about trying to sell it had been all wrong. I was trying to promote it directly to other bicycle racers. I traveled across the country, setting up a mobile display out of the back of my van. I would park my van on a street corner near the finish line and hand out flyers. I only sold about 20 units this way, and the conversion ratios were terrible. I hardly made enough money to break even on the trips. What I needed to do was get a booth at Interbike in Long Beach and sell directly to dealers and distributors.

That was a revelation. The trade show was my ticket. I was picking up momentum and confidence. This idea was going to work. I picked up the phone and called the people in California. The guy on the other end of the line laughed at me. He said I was crazy to think that I could get booth space three weeks before a show that sells out at least a year in advance.

I laughed back at him. *Too late to come to your trade show? More like too late to stop me.*

I made another call to the woodshop and had them build me a display that would simulate a floor and ceiling to display the bike racks at the show. A week later, I picked it up on the way out of town and loaded it into my van, along with my buddy Steve Sims, and we headed West. Look out, California, here we come.

This was the plan. I'd show up and see if there were any exhibitor booth cancellations. If not, I would attend the show and use it as another opportunity to research the media and the marketplace. It was a long drive, but we made it to the convention hotel just in time for the setup days of the trade show.

The salesperson had been right: I was crazy to think I could get a booth at the last moment. But I wasn't ready to give up and go home. I knew if I could just get in front of the right people and show what I had invented and patented, I would have a successful venture. So, here's what Steve and I did.

We waited until 2 a.m. on the last setup night and carried all our supplies and the trade show booth into the hotel's lobby area, where registration desks were set up. There, without permission, we set up our 10-by-10 booth outside the main doors of the convention expo hall. This was right across from the double doors entering the main trade show center, completely against the rules. I figured the worst they could do was kick us out.

The following day, we put on our suits, made our way to the lobby, turned on the lights on the booth, arranged all the flyers on a table, and looked ready for business. People started to filter into the registration area. Shockingly, not one person from the trade show staff even asked us what we thought we were doing.

This was a three-day show, and we thought we would certainly get kicked out at some point. We didn't. We also couldn't have asked for a better location because everybody entering and exiting the trade show floor had to walk directly by our booth. Other exhibitors complimented us on our booth location, and we had tons of foot traffic.

We handed out thousands of brochures about our products in the first two days, and we took wholesale orders for a few

CHAPTER THREE: THE SUPERPOWER OF PROSPERITY CONSCIOUSNESS

hundred bicycle storage units. We were excited, but a couple of hundred bike racks was way under our target, especially with the thousands of dealers at the trade show. Several bicycle magazines took pictures and interviewed us for new product reviews, and we received interest from import-export agencies, manufacturer's reps, chain stores, and specialty catalogs.

Traffic really slowed down by the end of the second day, and we thought the third day would be even slower. We would give it until noon to evaluate the traffic, and if it was slow, we would pack up and start the drive home early. The morning traffic was slow, and at 11:30 a.m., we started to pack boxes. Just as we started packing, a dealer walked up and handed us an order for 25 bike racks. We stopped packing, took the order, and thanked the man. A minute later, another dealer walked up and handed us his order, and then another and another and another order came rolling in. Steve and I were swamped, taking hundreds of orders from bicycle dealers and chain stores for the next five hours until the end of the show. We ended up with over $100,000 in new orders.

Of course, that big influx of orders created a whole host of other issues — production capacity, cash-flow concerns, growing business operations, infrastructure, staffing, publicity, marketing, packaging, and distribution, just to name a few — but we were up and running.

Had I left early as planned, I would have missed the number one opportunity to grow and develop my business. That business generated over $50 million in sales before I sold it in 1994. There are several important lessons here, the most important of which, I think, is don't listen to "I can't" self-talk and give up too soon. Don't wait too late, either. Don't be a Luther. Chase your own dreams. Stay positive. Stop pushing all the time. Try pulling. Carry a big stick.

THE POWER OF PERSISTENCE

Creating a prosperity consciousness is not a one-time activity. It's a lifelong practice. And it's not just about financial wealth. You can apply it, and you should, in all areas of your life. Say yes more often. Be good to yourself. Be positive. You'll be surprised to find how far that gets you in leadership, business, and life.

We are typically surrounded by so much negativity and influenced by our environment, the media, ethnicity, childhood upbringing, families, friends, coworkers, and society that this is not simply fix it and forget it. It takes effort, and regardless of what level of prosperity consciousness you reach, there are always new levels to reach for and achieve.

CHAPTER 3 KEY CONCEPTS:

- What do you want out of life?
- What are you doing to attract opportunities to you?
- Do you have a can-do attitude?

ACTION STEPS:

Developing Your Prosperity Consciousness Superpower

1. Make a list of all the people in your life that you spend time with on a regular basis. These might be family members, coworkers, associates, or friends. Give them a prosperity consciousness rating on a scale of 1 to 10, with 1 being lack-consciousness or generally negative and 10 being generally positive and highly supportive of positive activities, thoughts, and behaviors. Make a conscious effort to eliminate spending time with the negative people in your life and invest your time with people of prosperity consciousness. This exercise can be a real eye-opener.

2. Schedule time each week to read, watch, and/or listen to personal growth and development resources. You'll find that even resources that you may be familiar with in the past will have new insights as you grow and develop.

3. Reduce the number of hours you now spend watching TV, TikTok, Netflix, or other video distractions by up to 50% or more for at least 30 days...and notice how you'll naturally spend your time more productively.

4. Use your Hero Handbook to track your thoughts, feelings, actions, and results. Look for patterns of positivity and cynicism; identify your most common attitudes and outlooks. Take control of them.

CHAPTER FOUR:
SUPER SENSE

I LOVE BEING ON the water. I used to prefer it frozen. A hard, slick surface I could skate across. A platform to dominate, a place to compete, a track. I was a speed skater, always in a hurry. It took me a while to learn how to slow down, how to relax. It was the late 1990s, in fact. That's when I bought a boat, a 28-foot Bayliner cabin-cruiser, and put it in the warm waters of a small lake near the Flint Hills of Kansas called El Dorado. "The Golden Land" it means in Spanish. The lake was named after the nearby Kansas town that was named after the mission of explorer Francisco Vasquez de Coronado, who finally gave up his search not far from there for a fabled city of gold. He turned back. I did not. I jumped in. The water was fine.

When the first explorers arrived in the New World by ship, the natives did not see them coming because they had never seen a sailboat. They had no idea what they were looking at on the horizon. You would think that at least one of the natives would have turned to another and said, "What the hell is that? Should we be worried?"

It's easy to look back and laugh, but when was the last time you recognized a new idea? More importantly when you saw this new idea, this new opportunity, did you take any action? I think we've all had those moments in our lives where we had an idea — identified a need, puzzled out a solution, devised an invention, imagined an app — but never followed through. Then (what do you know?) we see it on the market a few years later and we kick ourselves. Someone else saw the same opportunity and seized upon it.

Identifying an opportunity is nice. Acting on an opportunity is a superpower.

FLOAT AN IDEA

As the saying goes, a boat is a hole in the water you throw money into. It's true. When I wasn't on the boat, I was shopping for accessories or fixing it. That's how I came to be at a boat show in Wichita, Kansas one Saturday morning, walking the aisles and checking out all the new gadgets. I had brought my son, Logan, along. He was five years old at the time. Like me, he loved all things nautical — except for those orange horse-collar life jackets we always made him wear. He hated those. That's why the sign at the boat show caught my eye: "FLOATING SWIMWEAR: PROTECT YOUR KIDS IN AND AROUND WATER," it read.

I walked right up to the booth and put my money down. I could see they were like tiny Lycra wetsuits with floatation material sewn into them. A simple idea that was well executed. A wonderful replacement for the uncomfortable life jackets. They were bright and colorful. Even Logan seemed excited about them. I didn't need to consider them any further. I was ready to make a deal.

"I'll take two," I said.

The guy behind the counter looked at me sideways.

"You want to know how much they cost first?"

CHAPTER FOUR: SUPER SENSE

Pish posh, my good man. Price? Please! I am not concerned with the cost of your items. I am concerned with keeping my child safe. The value of your product has been made abundantly clear to me and now I must have it. Why would I concern myself with the price? I would gladly pay it, whatever the amount.

That's what my manner looked like as I wrote him a check for $70.

Inside, I was thinking "What an idiot."

Okay. That might have been a bit harsh. He was simply a fellow who didn't know much about marketing or sales. You sell on value, not price. The value and benefit of his product — child safety and parental peace of mind — was immeasurable. As I walked away, I started to feel a little bad for him. Maybe I could help. I went back and offered him my business card.

"If you'd like to get some help on how to grow your business, let me know," I said.

I was in shorts and a T-shirt, not my usual business suit, but I explained to him that I was the CEO of an integrated marketing company and founder of a sporting goods manufacturing company. You know, the business I built with the bike racks. It was booming.

"Thanks, but no thanks," the guy said. "If I had a nickel for every guy like you who said that I could make millions, I'd have already made millions."

I decided that I had been right about the guy the first time.

Back at the lake, Logan loved the swimsuit. Wearing it made him feel like Superman. He could jump in the water, and his head would pop right up. He could comfortably swim and play in the water and he didn't even mind wearing it when he was on the boat or at the marina. Everyone felt safe. And everyone who saw Logan in the suit complimented him on how cool he looked. On top of that, they wanted to know where they could get one, too.

53

You hear that? That's an opportunity.

I went back to the boat show with my checkbook.

"I'll take the entire inventory," I said.

"What? Can't sell you all of 'em," the guy said to me, like I was the idiot. "There are two more days left in the boat show."

Sigh. Now I really felt sorry for him. Did he even understand the point of being in business?

We finally made a deal for all the suits he had on hand for $20 each. I loaded up my van with several boxes and drove back to the marina.

If this were a movie, what happened next would unfold in musical montage, set to a snappy song like "Walking on Sunshine" by Katrina and The Waves. A van pulls into the marina with the boxes of colorful swimsuits stacked in back. A smiling, eager fellow in summer wear (me) hops out and grabs a box. Then we cut to inside the marina store, where I am chatting with the manager at the counter, box in hand. The manager seems skeptical but willing. Cut to him watching over my shoulder as I remove all the potato chips from the top shelf next to the register and replace them with the floating swimsuits for kids. Cut to a close-up of a hand-drawn sign being taped to the shelf: "$50 each while supplies last." Then there are the several quick shots in a row of the swimsuits being grabbed from the shelf, money changing hands at the register, repeatedly, moms and dads and sunburned uncles making an impulse purchase at the counter for their nephews until the last suit is gone. Seeing the empty shelf, the manager nods his head in quiet approval. He'd taken a chance and made out like a bandit, earning a fat percentage of every sale. His face says "Well, I'll be darned." And ... scene.

"You sold all of those suits already?" is how the next scene starts at the swimwear office. I've decided this guy should be played by the guy who played "Booger" in all of those

CHAPTER FOUR: SUPER SENSE

"Revenge of the Nerds" movies. Grouchy, awkward, intelligent, well-meaning, but without a lot of cool or common sense. He's looking at me like he can't believe it. "That was an entire year's inventory," he says.

Maybe some people just aren't cut out to be entrepreneurs, or they just don't know what they don't know. I hadn't come to buy more swimsuits. I explained to him that I was serious about helping him grow his business, and he agreed to another meeting with me to discuss the venture in more detail.

I thought about how many marinas, boating stores, and pool and spa dealers there were in the United States and the world. The floating swimwear idea was a winner. But the inventor needed help marketing his product in the right places to the right people. I had some ideas and the experience to help him pull it off.

Later, he came to my office and I gave him the tour of our production facility for the bicycle storage systems and shared stories about how I had built a multimillion-dollar sporting goods business and specialized in helping other people turn their ideas into reality. After we talked for several hours, he concluded that he really wanted help getting investment capital to grow his business. He hired me to write a business and marketing plan and prepare a presentation for venture capitalists and potential investors. I wrote the plan, and within two weeks, we had generated over $150,000 in new cash capital for his business. He was happy, and while I tried to explain to him that although the new cash seemed like a lot of money, it might be just enough for him to go bankrupt. My plan called for almost double that amount, but he decided he would go forward with the plan on his own.

Fast-forward a few months. I was busy with my own projects and business ventures but decided to follow up to see how Floating Swimwear was doing with the new plan. I called the owner, and he was not happy. He was close to bankruptcy, his wife was upset with him, and his investors were angry.

"What happened?" I said, confused. "Did you follow the plan we laid out?"

"Well, not exactly. I tried something different."

My plan called for increasing the manufacturing capabilities, changing production from girls' and boys' suits to unisex suits, packaging them for distribution to pool & spa stores and mass merchants, generating free publicity for new product reviews and special interest stories, and developing new branding and a multichannel plan for different channels of distribution. This plan was developed using my research and years of experience and expertise in selling products and services that I had patented and developed.

What did Booger do? He made an infomercial.

SINK OR SWIM

Instead of following my plan, the inventor of Floating Swimwear invested $75,000 to create an infomercial to sell his suits direct on late-night TV and cable. He took the other $75,000 and bought remnant commercial airtime (the advertising time slots sold at a discount because other advertisers don't want it). That can work for certain products, but it doesn't work for the demographic he was trying to reach to encourage them to buy floating swimwear for their children. In short, most moms and dads are not up all night watching television. They have work in the morning.

All his money was gone, and he had sold 36 suits. Hardly a profitable venture. I can see where he was convinced to try that strategy, but there were too many flaws for it ever to work.

The advertising salespeople had convinced him that he would be advertising only in demographic marketplaces that had a high capacity of pool owners and customers around

CHAPTER FOUR: SUPER SENSE

water. They didn't explain to him that while they gave him a discount on the ad slots, those ads would be running at 3 a.m. Worse yet, instead of testing small to find out the right combination and sales conversion strategies, he opted to buy a more extensive advertising package to get discounts. In the end, the infomercial strategy was a financial disaster.

He asked for more help.

"You spent all your money, and now you can't afford my help," is what I could have said. But I didn't. I love a challenge. And I don't give up. So instead, I asked myself some questions.

"How can we generate revenue and manage his debt while growing the company at the same time?" The strategy of asking the right questions just seemed obvious. I think the problem with most people is that they either ask the wrong questions or they give up too soon and don't ask any questions at all. If you're struggling with a challenge or problem, step back from the problem to get a clearer perspective, pose new questions, and allow your brain to help you come up with solutions.

It was still obvious to me that floating swimwear was a great product with great potential. The question was how we could tap that potential effectively. I offered him a deal where I would help him get his business back on track that would be mutually beneficial for both of us. The deal that I outlined for him was that we would move his business operations into our offices and production facility, and all I wanted in return was $2 commission per swimsuit sold. He could add the $2 to the cost of goods and pay me monthly on units sold for the product line's life. He jumped at the deal, but he was still skeptical.

"I sure hope you know what you're doing," he said.

"You let me worry about that," I said.

I followed the original business plan. It really came down to positioning the product correctly in the marketplace and improving distribution channels. Prior to working with us,

57

his initial strategy was to sell them at consumer boating shows, and his next strategy was to sell at retail direct using infomercials. Both strategies created lackluster sales (and that's being generous).

His main benefit message was to save kids' lives and give parents peace of mind. That was the end result of the product, but that wasn't the benefit to the dealer market as outlined in the business plan. Remember the marina manager? He didn't see lifesavers; he saw dollar signs when he agreed to move his potato chips to make way for the swimsuits. The benefit to dealers and chain stores was to create an instant profit center and increase sales from impulse purchases during checkout. The obvious changes were to target the marketing message to the specific target market and to use the appropriate marketing method.

This strategy may sound simple, but it has been a foundational strategy in the success of many new product launches, new business ventures, and marketing campaigns. Suppose you have success in your business or the company you work for. In that case, it's because you have the right combination of benefit message (the why) to a specific target market (the who) delivered using an appropriate marketing method (the how).

Here's another musical montage of what happened next, this one set to "We're in the Money."

A contract is drawn up at a desk, and then we cut to a shot of an airplane taking off. Cut to bustling scenes at wholesale trade shows on both coasts. Now a close up of orders being filed, stacks and stacks of them. Now we're in a pool supply store and a clerk is stocking the swimwear. There's Booger smoking a cigar. The seasons come and go and the calendar pages peel by on the screen. Within a few short years, retail sales reached over $10 million, and Floating Swimwear, Inc., grows to over 100 employees. We cut back to my boat on El Dorado Lake, now golden with the setting sun. Logan, laughing, launches himself safely over the side. I beam at my boy in the water.

And ... scene.

THE POWER OF TELEPATHY

There was gold near El Dorado all along. Opportunity is everywhere, in fact. You don't need to know where to look so much as *how* to look — and then what to do when you see it. Take heed and take action. That's the takeaway here. That's the superpower.

Although this story may sound unique, stories of success like this are everywhere. Have you ever seen a new product and said, "Hey, I thought of that idea years ago!" I believe that each one of us gets several great ideas each week, but unless you practice and condition yourself to write those ideas down, they will vanish from your mind like the dreams you don't remember when you wake up.

A big difference between successful people and everyone else is that successful people capture their ideas. You don't have any excuses for not recording your own good ideas. Most likely, you have a smartphone and you can easily leave yourself a message, text yourself a message, or use an app to record your ideas. Do it!

CHAPTER 4 KEY CONCEPTS:

- Identify opportunities.
- Capture your ideas.
- Act on those opportunities and ideas.

ACTION STEPS:

Develop the Superpower Mindset

1. Use your Hero Handbook to record at least one opportunity that you identify each day. At the end of the week, look over this list. You should have a minimum of seven opportunities identified for potential action. What were you doing at the time you identified the opportunity?

2. What did you do (or could you have done) to act on that opportunity when you identified it? If you didn't act, what held you back? If you did act, what was the outcome?

PART 2:
REFRAME

CHAPTER FIVE:
SUCCESS-RAY VISION

Iron Man, Invisible Woman, Captain America. Sure, those superheroes do fantastic feats and are fun comic book characters. But Harold von Braunhut was the real deal.

We don't talk much about Harold today. There are no Harold Halloween costumes, no movies. But his heroism was on display in every comic book on the rack from the 1950s well into the 1990s. His superpower was capturing your imagination. He'd do that and then add value to your life by adding amazement — all while earning a fair profit for his efforts. The guy was a mad genius and mail-order business master.

Every comic book adventure ended with an appearance from Harold and his wild inventions. Sea-Monkeys, for example. He "invented" those. They were neither monkeys nor were they from the sea. They were brine shrimp collected from lake beds. He sold them in the back of comic books by the billions, trillions maybe. (They were so tiny, who could count them all?) You've seen the ads. THE REAL LIVE FUN PETS YOU GROW YOURSELF, the headlines promised. The full-color ads featured a happy nuclear family of Sea-Monkeys — mom, dad, and two kids — pose in the bowl as if they were being photographed on a beach. Mom is a pretty blonde wearing lipstick. Dad has a hand on his son's shoulder. "Gee, dad. Isn't this swell?" the boy shrimp seems to be saying. "It sure is, buddy. It sure is."

That's not the only big seller Harold came up with. He held 195 patents for inventions, including baby doll eyes that close. He also peddled Amazing Hair-Raising Monsters, Crazy Crabs, and Invisible Goldfish. The "fish" shipped in an empty glass bowl along with a guarantee that they "would remain permanently invisible or your money back."

He also sold X-Ray Specs. These came with the promise to make the invisible *visible*. "Scientific optical principle really works," the ads read. "Imagine — you put on the X-Ray Specs and hold your hand in front of you. You seem to be able to look right through the flesh and see the bones underneath. Look at your friends. Is that really his body you see under his clothes?"

The answer is no, it was not his body you saw under his clothes. Still, you saw what wasn't apparent before. The mystery made it thrilling. What were you seeing?

WHAT DO YOU SEE?

One of the first steps to success is to get clear on what you want to do, be, have, or become. Do you really know? Whether you're reading this for improvements in your personal life, leadership, or business success, it's important to have a clear destination.

You don't need X-Ray Specs; you need what I call Success-Ray Vision.

Do you know what success looks like, I mean, really looks like for YOU? If the answer is no, don't panic. I'm going to reveal a few strategies to help you get clarity.

The X-Ray Specs worked as advertised. Harold carefully billed them as a "hilarious optical illusion." When you wear them, you do see the world in a new way. You are looking through feathers. Those feathers are sandwiched inside the cardboard lenses. When you look through the pinholes in the lenses, objects appear to have a fuzzy outer glow, sort of like an X-ray image. You are not really seeing through walls, your hand, or a dress, of course. You are not seeing through anything but the feathers. Still, the effect is fun as it fools the eye and the mind.

Success-Ray Vision is the opposite. It's about looking inward. It's about turning the picture you have in your mind into a reality. It is a way to make the invisible *truly* visible. There's no trick to it, only believing in yourself, setting goals, and taking action.

DON'T FOOL YOURSELF

Ugh. Goals. I can hear you sighing from here. You have surely been made to set goals by this time in your life, either by a parent, coach, employer, or mentor. It's been explained to you, or maybe even demonstrated, how goal setting works and how you can achieve what you set your mind to if you just apply yourself and ... blah, blah, blah.

All of that is true, but it's not worth explaining again to you as if you were 10 years old. But what IS worth repeating is that it's not what you know, it's how well you execute. The power of goal setting is that it focuses you. You gain a sense of direction. You work toward an end point. And when you set them correctly, you will know that the work you are putting in has a purpose and clear reward. That's the most important part of the goal, in fact — the why. It doesn't get talked about enough in some systems, such as S.M.A.R.T. goals. But the *why* is where your goals should begin and end. The *why* is the everything. What you want is an outcome, of course. But why do you want that outcome? The outcome is usually an achievement or a procurement. You want a new job or a better car. That's tangible.

The *why* is emotional. You want to live a better life, to look and feel like a million bucks, to drive into the sunset in style.

WHAT IT REALLY LOOKS LIKE

Here is what the process of goal setting should look like. Start by writing what you want in detail. It's important to stretch yourself. Think big.

Examples:

- ▶ You want to be driving a new BMW within six months.

- ▶ Earn a promotion at your job as the youngest vice president in company history.

- ▶ Looking sharp in a suit that fits better because you've lost 22 lbs.

- ▶ Become a thought leader in your industry, earning seven figures a year.

Now think about *why* you want them. Remember, the *why* is the most important element.

Examples:

- ▶ I want to feel cool in my car and project an image of success.

- ▶ To achieve significance, recognition, and financial rewards.

- ▶ Feeling fit will give me increased confidence, energy, and appeal.

- ▶ To make an impact and make the world a better place.

DEFEAT THE BULLY

If you have a strong enough *why*, you will figure out the *how*. There's another famous ad from comic books that applies here. Like the Sea-Monkeys ad, it is a beach scene. But the shrimp in this one is a puny-looking guy in swim trunks. He's got a pretty gal on his arm. Trouble is, there's a well-built bully in the other corner with his eyes on her. "Hey, Skinny!" the bully says. "Your ribs are showing!" The rest unfolds in comic strip panels. There is a scuffle in the sand, the little guy loses and goes home and vows never to let that happen again. "Darn it! I'm tired of being a skinny scarecrow." He sends away for Charles Atlas' bodybuilding course. In the next panel, he's buff and admiring himself in the mirror. "Boy, it didn't take long. What a build. Now I will take care of that bully!" He does, of course. And wins the heart of the girl and the admiration of the beachgoers in the background. "What a man!" they all say.

It's easy to dismiss the ad today as a dopey example of toxic masculinity. But it was effective at the time. More importantly, what Charles Atlas was selling was real. It was no illusion. It actually worked. What you got in the mail was a pamphlet with diet and exercise tips. If you followed them, you would see results. It was just a matter of how much work you were willing to put in on a consistent basis to improve yourself.

Was it muscles that the kid wanted? Not really. What he really wanted was to defeat the bully and feel better about himself. That was a powerful motivator. That was his *why*.

GET REAL

I've never played basketball on a team of any level in my life, so it is not likely that I will sign with the New York Knicks. Nor is it realistic to think that if I run east that I'll ever see a sunset. I would be going in the wrong direction. Setting either of those as goals would be ridiculous — I'd only let myself down.

This is important to keep in mind because each time you set a goal and miss the mark, you can lower your self-esteem. If you lower your self-esteem too much, you give up or fail to try at all. As you refer to your goals list, ask yourself if you truly believe that your goal is realistic, and if not, why not? What would you have to do, have, or become to make your goal more realistic? Can you become the type of person who has the attitude, aptitude, discipline, and consistency to reach your goal? This is where having an unrealistic expectation or conflicting goal sets you up for potential failure.

Be honest with yourself. Are you really going to earn $10 million in 10 days? If you will not stop eating chocolate and fast food and hate exercise, are you really going to lose 10 pounds? The reality is that you will not — unless, of course, you change your mindset and behavior, which is entirely possible (and what this book is about). You just need to get enough leverage and the proper strategy to replace the old behaviors with new behaviors.

MEASURE UP

A business that operates without the proper measurements is doomed to crash and fail. Imagine driving the new BMW that was listed as a goal in the example above. It handles like a dream, but you are in a nightmare. For some reason, the windows are painted black, and you can't see the road. There are no gauges inside to tell which way you are going or how fast. Still, you step on the gas. Are you crazy? How far do you think you will go before you crash?

You would be surprised how many small and large businesses do just that by failing to implement and pay attention to their feedback systems and reports. They're not checking their gauges. The mileposts are flying by. Maybe. They have no idea how many and they will probably hit one soon and come to a halt anyway. You may have heard, "If you don't know where you're going, how are you going to get there?" It's a good question. I would go you one better and say, "If you don't know where you're going AND have measurements in place to see if you're on track, you won't reach your destination."

Sets mileposts toward each of your goals. Apply metrics. When you measure your progress, it helps you stay on track and motivates you to continue the journey. Refer to your company's performance and finance reports. Check your savings account balance. Step on the scale. The numbers don't lie. If the numbers are not where they need to be — if you are not where you need to be — make course corrections.

THE POWER OF MAGNETISM

Here's the whole key to settings goals, no matter which system you use or what you are working toward. Want ... something! Want it by a specific date. Want it bad. Want it because it will make you feel a certain way. That's what keeps us all going. That's what motivated the kid on the beach. He wanted to beat the bully. And that's what motivated those millions of teenagers to buy what Harold was selling. They weren't looking for a small packet of brine shrimp or cardboard and feathers. They wanted what would transform their lives by giving them a superpower, like X-ray vision or dominion over a cute family of sea creatures that they could raise and train to follow their commands. They would send in their money and check their mailbox every day until it arrived. You don't have to wait. You can see to it yourself right now. You already have Success-Ray

Vision. Use it to set your sights, get clear about what you want, and turn your dreams into goals. That's how you make them come true.

CHAPTER 5 KEY CONCEPTS:

- What does success look like for you?
- Can you name the 'what' and the 'why' of your goals?
- How will you know you're on track to reaching your goals?

ACTION STEPS:

Goal Setting

1. List all the goals you want to achieve, both short-term (this month or year) and long-term (next three to five years and beyond).

2. Put them into specific categories or roles. For example, personal, professional, relationships, spiritual, wealth, health, and so on…

3. Connect your goal to your big "WHY." Write out what you have to gain and lose by not attaining each goal to ensure that you have the proper leverage and motivation to reach the specific goal.

CHAPTER SIX:
ADDING VALUE IS A SUPERPOWER

Batman is not for everyone. He broods. Such a dark figure. Sure, he has lots of cool gadgetry and gets the crime-fighting job done and Gotham City seems safe … for now. But would it kill the guy to smile once in a while?

Think about the last server you tipped really well, above and beyond your normal percentage. It's probably because she went above and beyond the typical server duties in a noticeable way. She was sunny, first of all, and wearing a real smile. She was attentive to your table without being too present. You never lacked for water or bread. She recommended a great dessert. All fine and what you would expect. But here's where she excelled. When the meal was over, she brought you a mint. "You know what? Actually, have two mints," she said, conspiratorially handing them to you as if she would get in trouble if anyone saw but you just seem so nice, and she can't help it. "They're great," she whispers. "You'll love them."

Hear that? That's the sound of a good tip on the way.

Batman could have been just as efficient, maybe even faster, but he wouldn't have made you feel special. He would fire those mints at you like throwing stars and then disappear into the kitchen. "I'm Batman," is all that he would say. But we already knew that.

The server was efficient AND kind AND generous. Batman was efficient but kind of a jerk. The server "added value" by delivering a fantastic customer experience. That's a superpower.

Adding more value to increase your success relates to many areas of your life, so whether you are a waiter, a business owner, an executive, or part of a team, you can benefit from asking yourself, "How can I add more value?"

ADD VALUE, MAKE A PROFIT

Many people in business focus on external factors that they don't have any control over, like government regulations, the economy, inflation, and negative people. But if you really want to use your superpower, focus on what you can control and ask questions related to how you can be of service to others. That's where the profit is.

Here is a way to get started. Map out the customer journey, look at every touchpoint you have with the customer, and then ask yourself, "How can I add more value?" Look at operations, or shipping, or the product, or the service, or accounting, or billing. Look at every facet, any touchpoint you have with the customer, and ask yourself this: How do I improve the experience? How do I improve the customer experience? Improving the customer experience will add more value. You'll see results when you do.

ADD VALUE, EARN MORE INCOME

Again, unsuccessful people don't think that way. They just want the result without thinking about how to they can be of service to get there. Well, the path to get there is by asking better questions. What are the skill sets, abilities, and talents that would add more value to others in your personal and professional life if you developed? There is no such thing as job security, only skills security. So, develop your skills and you'll always have opportunities. Determine the skillsets that make you invaluable to the company you are at right now. Sharpen or spotlight them every chance you get, which will help you excel in your organization or future opportunities.

ADD VALUE, BE MORE LOVED

We all should focus on adding more value and becoming better people in all areas of our lives. We can add value as parents. How do you create great experiences with your kids? How do you create an educational experience? How can you be a better partner or friend? It may seem touchy-feely, but relationships are vital, and when nurtured they improve the quality of your life. We should all have the goal to grow as human beings. That has nothing to do with how much we earn, own, or influence — it has to do with how much we give. I love this anonymous quote, "Give without remembering... receive without forgetting."

LIGHT A FIRE

The more you give of yourself — your time, talent, energy, expertise, and kindness — the more you will get back in return for yourself, and the more value you will create for others. "Life gives to the givers... and takes from the takers," as the saying goes. That's more than feel-good sloganeering. That's the human experience and evolution in action. Someone once spent more time than the other guy rubbing sticks together and became an expert. He discovered how to make a fire with what he had on hand rather than wait for lightning to strike.

And then he shared the idea and made everyone's life better. Imagine how popular he was around the cave. Batman would be jealous.

So, yes, life gives to the givers. Sounds nice and makes you feel righteous to think that way of yourself. Now, you can sew that on a pillow and relax in your bat cave and feel good about yourself, or you can get busy applying the principle, do some good in the world, and reap the rewards.

"QUICK, ROBIN, TO THE ... SUCCESS LIBRARY"

Remember that Batman is just a guy who developed special skills. He wasn't born a superhero. There is no radiation accident in his origin story. He just worked harder than the rest to be a good guy, developing the fighting, climbing, and deductive reasoning skills he needed to outsmart the bad guy. The Bat Cave plays a large role in his success. It's more than a garage for the Batmobile. It's the Dark Knight's library and lab. It's where he works to solve the latest cryptic code from the Riddler, or to prove once and for all that the Joker is not funny. He has resources there beyond his butler and boy ward. There's a computer, shelves of references books, maps, laboratory testing equipment, and high-tech gadgets.

Batman, in other words, has a Success Library. You should, too, if you hope to develop your skills and add value.

In an earlier chapter, I asked you to identify the skill sets necessary for success in the different roles of your life, like being a parent, a spouse, a friend, a colleague, a business owner, a leader, and a coworker. How did you do? By rating yourself, you can identify focus areas and find gaps for improvement.

Once you have the list, the next step is to add resources to your Success Library and your brain. Think about what courses, consultants, or how-to training resources will best help you bridge your value gap. You're building more than a bookshelf. Your Success Library is any and all the resources you need, in whatever medium (mentors, consultants, audiobooks, podcasts, videos, online courses) you can find to support your superpower journey. I'm honored that you've added this book to your success library. Be a giver... get a copy of this book for your team and those you care about, too.

Success leaves clues. You can either learn from your own experience or from other people's experiences. Why re-invent the wheel when you can shorten your learning curve through the guidance of successful people?

As a business, you'll improve engagement and retention when you give your staff opportunities for knowledge and skills growth by providing Success Library resources. It could be onboarding videos about your company's culture, standard operating procedures, or the customer experience you cultivate. Or it could be about the mentors you tap or the experts you bring to your organization for skills training.

For example, when I speak at an organization, I become a part of its Success Library. I've added value, given them tools, techniques, templates, guidelines, formulas, and stories they can relate to with actionable takeaways.

Everyone can benefit from a Success Library. Business owners, Students. Parents. Middle managers looking to make a move up. There is no end of information out there to tap into to gain insights and glean value. We are in the age of instant information. There are no excuses. Here are a few additional resources to get you started: Books with Amazon, LinkedIn Learning courses, YouTube Videos, Audible, and Kindle books. Or find a mentor (a subject we'll talk about in another chapter). But don't bother asking Batman. That guy could work on his people skills.

CHAPTER 6 KEY CONCEPTS:

- Add value to increase success
- Create your success library

ACTION STEPS:

An Exercise to Develop and Increase Your Value

Pick one goal you want to focus on. Identify at least 20 positive benefits (value) of this goal to your customers and 20 positive benefits (value) that will result for you or your business.

- If this is a personal goal, what is the value that you will receive personally by completing this goal? What is the value that others will receive when you achieve your goal?

- If this is a business growth goal, what is the value to your customers (benefits they will receive) from utilizing your services or purchasing your product? And in return for offering your customers this great value, what is the resulting value offered to the growth of your organization.

Now compare the two lists you just created for value. If the value list is longer for the benefits, *you* will receive than the list for your customers, do not expect to be successful or enjoy profitable sales. You need to increase the value, or perceived value, to your customers for them to buy from your business.

CHAPTER SEVEN:
THE POWER OF IDEAS

SOME MORNINGS, I put on my top hat and tails and stroll the avenue searching for a poor street urchin. When one reaches out from the gutter with their grubby little paw to beg for a handout, I strike it down with my cane.

"You're not out of money," I scold. "You're out of ideas."

Harsh? Perhaps. But how else will they learn?

Before the hate mail starts coming in, I'm NOT talking about homeless people or social issues; I'm making the point with the cartoon version of how I imagine it comes across when I share this tough-love truth about money with people. But it is true: There is no such thing as a lack of money; there is only a lack of ideas.

If you want to earn more money, activate your creative thinking to generate more ideas. There is no shortage of money in the world. You just have to find ways to be more innovative to add the value that creates the exchange of currency.

"Fine then, Mr. Moneybags. How do I get my hands on more ideas?"

I'm glad you asked, good sir. That I can help you with.

ON BEING INNOVATIVE AND CREATIVE

Innovation was once someone's new idea of what to call a new idea. But now, everyone calls their new ideas "innovations." How innovating! Being creative means finding new ways to do it, say it, or solve it. Start by not following the herd and "innovating." In fact, stop putting so much pressure on yourself. Just create. That's all creativity is ... the act of creating. You can do that. Anyone can do that.

Many people put being creative on a pedestal and think it is beyond their abilities or that they just weren't born creative. Don't be fooled. Being creative is simply thinking and tinkering. Most best-selling authors, for example, would tell you that it wasn't their brains that got them there — it was their butts. They planted them in a chair and did the work.

Now, while there are some savants with what seems to be exceptional talents, most innovations come through practice, failing, persistence and patience. You don't need natural talent to come up with great ideas to improve your life, leadership, or business — you just need to put your butt into it.

CREATIVE EXCUSES

I hear it all the time. People shrug and say, "I'm just not creative." Not true. It's an excuse they're making for not putting in the effort. It's also a fear of being judged or fear of failure. I get that. It can hurt to have an idea shot down. But what's worse is never offering one. You must be willing to fail, take risks, and look a bit foolish in the attempt sometimes if you hope to be bold. That holds a lot of people back who would rather play it safe.

It's easy to go through life avoiding the new, the strange, the uncomfortable. Think about it. You probably have many routines that you haven't changed for a long time: what time you get up in the morning, the route you drive to work, the food you eat, the shows you watch. There is certainly a purpose for these routines, and without them, our lives would be in chaos, but when it comes to idea generation, you should be willing to shake it up now and then.

WHAT WILL HAPPEN IF YOU …?

- ▶ Take a different route to work tomorrow
- ▶ Move your ring to a different finger
- ▶ Cross-train your brain
- ▶ Sit in a new place for meetings
- ▶ Startup a conversation with a stranger
- ▶ Sleep on a different side of the bed
- ▶ Brush your teeth with your other hand
- ▶ Listen to Reggae music

Here is my best guess on what will happen: You will see, feel, and hear new things. That's a great start toward opening yourself up to new ideas.

It's challenging to be creative if you're constantly having the same experiences, always following the rules, afraid to make mistakes, or only focused on getting a solution and moving on. If you think there's only one solution, then you will stop looking as soon as you find one that seems good enough. There might have been a better one if you kept looking. We all should never stop looking and learning in life. The world is full of possibilities. Remember, anyone can be more creative The people who do it with the most ease are explorers.

They share these traits:

- ▶ They're curious about the world

- ▶ Avid readers
- ▶ Delighted by novelty
- ▶ Risk takers and rebels
- ▶ Critical thinkers
- ▶ Travelers and adventurers

Creative types enjoy a rich diet of stimulation, variety, and situations. They are exposed to a steady stream of new opinions, languages, cultures, and attitudes. They see a much broader spectrum of society, people in general, and the world.

How nice for them. You might not have the time in your life right now to explore the world, as you are running a business or a team and that takes all of your attention. That doesn't mean you are not in search of new ideas or solutions. You might lean on your team to be idea generators to help drive revenue growth or improve your processes so you can add value and increase profits. So, let's explore effective ways right here and now to help you encourage your team to improve their strategic thinking to yield breakthroughs for your business.

DEVELOP CREATIVE CONFIDENCE

We talked about what holds most people back from being creative — the fear of looking foolish in front of friends, family, teammates, of being shot down in the boardroom. That's an obstacle that can be overcome. You can't manufacture a thicker skin for your crew, but you can manage the process so that being creative always feels safe.

Think of new ideas as bubbles. They're beautiful, delicate, and may easily burst. When you're brainstorming, you want your team to blow bubbles and delight in them as they dance in the air. If you start popping them, it's going to get messy. Let them float. Don't remark on them right away, even if they're good. Just enjoy them for now. Encourage more. Fill the room if you can. Fast. Brainstorming sessions are most effective when brief but eventful, like storms. I recommend no more than 15- to-20-minute sessions. Assign a neutral facilitator. Select one of your team members to run the session if you're the CEO or manager. Remember, no criticism during brainstorming. If someone tosses out an idea and you say, "Hey, that's great!" or "No, that won't work," then you are going to limit the flow of ideas. Think wacky and go for quantity versus quality. Practice piggybacking on previous ideas.

If your group is reluctant to share their ideas in public openly, then you can pass out post-it notepads or index cards — all the same color, or it defeats the purpose — or have them prepare their ideas in writing before the session. No names, of course. This keeps it about the ideas, not the people who produced them, their feelings, or egos.

Once you've gathered several ideas, the next step is to clarify, categorize, discuss, eliminate items, and prioritize your list. But that's all paperwork and process. You'll get to that. Let's keep blowing bubbles, keep the ideas flowing for now.

CREATIVE PROMPTS

A great way to stimulate creative thinking is by asking open-ended questions. The kinds of questions you want to ask are what-if and possibility questions like:

- ▶ But if it was possible, how could it be done?
- ▶ In what ways might I (we) attract new customers?
- ▶ In what ways might I become more creative?
- ▶ What if we started over from ground zero and did it another way?

THE SCAMPER TECHNIQUE

You can't always invite imagination into the room and let it run wild — that can be unproductive. Create a reason for your team to innovate; give them a place to put new ideas. When you apply parameters to creative exercises, you can get surprising results. Even if they're not about your product or service, prompting creative solutions is good training for your team. One way to do that is by asking your team members to look at a familiar situation in a new way using the SCAMPER technique. This was first developed by Alex Osborne and later refined by Bob Eberle to develop more creativity in the workplace. It's a helpful technique for discovering solutions to a challenge. SCAMPER is an acronym for seven different ways you can view an idea.

S–Substitute

C–Combine

A–Adapt

M–Modify

P–Put to other uses

E–Eliminate

R–Reverse/Rearrange

The process may seem silly at first, but it's the kind of technique that brings bold, daring, and imaginative ideas to the surface.

An example of SCAMPER using an umbrella:

Substitute: Use a plastic bag stretched over a wire coat hanger.

Combine: Add a radio and digital clock to the handle.

Adapt: Make it useful for joggers by attaching it to the body.

Modify: Make it big enough to cover several people at once.

Put to other uses: Use the tip for poking holes or picking up scrap paper.

Eliminate: Take away the metal spokes that are always bending.

Reverse: Have the umbrella fold up instead of down to catch the water.

THE CREATIVITY UTILITY BELT

One of the greatest techniques for getting creative juices flowing is idea mapping, a.k.a., mind mapping. This process is inherently creative by its nature. So, what is this process? Mind mapping is a concept coined by Tony Buzan many years ago and has been adapted by different people throughout the years. Mind mapping is an accelerated learning technique that allows you to capture details and generate ideas faster, recall information quicker, and retain content longer.

Mind mapping is an integral part of our business operations. We use it during consultations, planning marketing campaigns, capturing ideas from brainstorming sessions, developing workflow processes and website design structure, and training and development.

Mind maps allow you to work visually and are less restrictive than traditional methods. This is not to say that the concept of creating an outline is not effective. They are just different techniques with different purposes. We start with the mind map and then, when necessary, move it to an outline format.

If you're new to mind mapping, I suggest you start practicing on paper first, as the process of physically writing and capturing your thoughts in visual patterns is proven to engage your creative juices. There are several mind mapping software programs and smartphone apps. We use software from MindManager.com, a cloud-based solution. See the *Hero Handbook* for how to create a mind map on your own.

CHAPTER 7 KEY CONCEPTS:

- Innovate and create.
- Use the SCAMPER creativity technique.
- Create your mind map for success.

ACTION STEPS:

Steps For Mind Mapping Success:

1. Start with a blank piece of paper and **make a circle in the center** of the page and write the main topic or area of focus in the center.

2. Create **branches** off the center circle and write an idea or category with simple stick figures or simple sketches to help illustrate the concepts. For example, when I'm idea mapping a marketing campaign, I have branches for the goals (target), ideal market (happy face), benefits & features (dollar signs), and methods (stars).

3. Use **associations** — Use lines, arrows, colors, and sketches to indicate relationships and connections between ideas.

4. Use **emphasis** — Use images, colors, dimensions, and size to reflect relative importance.

5. Leave **space** — Allow yourself room to add new branches and subtopics.

6. **Practice** — As you read the rest of this book, create a mind map to capture your ideas and action steps.

ACTION STEPS FOR DEVELOPING YOUR INNOVATION AND CREATIVITY SUPERPOWERS

1. Select your favorite method for capturing your ideas and start today.

2. Integrate idea mapping in your personal and professional lives.

3. Cross-train yourself by getting out of your comfort zone and experiencing new processes, places, and people.

CHAPTER EIGHT:
CRITICAL THINKING: USING YOUR SUPER SMARTS

The Incredible Hulk is an incredible idiot. He reacts without thinking. Then what happens? He always regrets it. He's self-aware enough to know this, but that never prevents him from throwing a guy through a wall anyway.

"Don't make me angry," David Banner, the Hulk's alter ego, will say. "You won't like me when I'm angry."

But then someone goes and makes him angry, and Banner transforms into a raging, green muscle head — again. "Hulk smash," he roars. And then he smashes. Big surprise.

If your usual mode of response is to react, you may spend your time feeling like you're spinning out of control, making poor, fear-based decisions, and you may be living your life in survival mode ("Hulk smash") rather than success mode. Developing your critical thinking is key to making decisions that better your life and business. That's why the Hulk was never a hero of mine. I prefer men of reason, like Benjamin Franklin. His superpower, critical thinking, turned him into a green $100 bill.

BE LIKE BEN

Most of us know Ben Franklin's story. He was a founding father, of course. He was also a publisher and inventor. We can thank the man for coming up with bifocals, swim fins, cabin stoves, lightning rods, and many of the words we still use today when talking about electricity — battery, charge, positive, and negative. He was always thinking, re-thinking, and referencing his Success Library. His shelves grew so tall he had to invent a way to fetch the books beyond his reach, so he created a long pole with mechanical fingers.

Here was a guy who thought it all through and then took action. He thought it through so much that he invented a process to make his thinking more efficient and effective.

It looked like this:

"My way is to divide half a sheet of paper by a line into two columns; writing over the one Pro and over the other Con," Franklin wrote to a friend. "Then during three- or four-days' consideration, I put down under the different heads short hints of the different motives, that at different times occur to me, for or against the measure. When I have thus got them altogether in one view, I endeavor to estimate their respective weights; and where I find two, one on each side, that seem equal, I strike them both out. If I judge some two reasons con equal to some three reasons pro, I strike out five; and thus proceeding, I find where the balance lies; and if after a day or two of further consideration, nothing new that is of importance occurs on either side, I come to a determination accordingly."

That's right. He created the pros and cons list, a process to apply critical thinking to all his endeavors.

THE (NOT) EVIL GENIUS OF LOGIC

Critical thinking is more than dashing off a list, of course, it's an analytical way of approaching and making decisions. It uses logic to look at situations, evaluate the different options, and then make conclusions based on the best evidence at the time. Leaders who strive to remove emotion from the equation and take the time to consider all angles and possible outcomes ultimately make better decisions for their business.

Developing your critical thinking superpower is a key strategy for success in all areas of our lives. Taking the time to analyze your different options quickly, so you can *act* rather than react will ensure you're making great choices that move you along in the direction you want to go. Remember what happens to the Hulk every time he reacts instead of acts. His alter ego wakes up in the rubble, his clothes torn to ribbons, and he has to slink out of there before the authorities arrive and ask, "What were you thinking?"

CHAPTER 8 KEY CONCEPTS:

- Develop your critical thinking
- Be like Ben (and write your pros and cons)
- Analyze your options

ACTION STEPS:

Tips to Improve Your Critical Thinking Skills

1. Approach new problems with an open mind. Do your thinking on paper or leverage the superpower of mind mapping that I mentioned earlier.

2. Define your desired outcome.

3. Get a clear understanding of the problem you're trying to solve. Aim to see the situation as it is, not making it better or worse than it really is.

4. Consider the situation from all angles and perspectives.

5. Do your research. Who else has struggled with a similar situation and solved it? What can you discover or model from those other situations?

CHAPTER EIGHT: CRITICAL THINKING: USING YOUR SUPER SMARTS

6. Challenge your assumptions. Are they based on fact, emotions, or rational thought?

7. Define at least three options. If you feel you have no choice, then you create more stress, and your brain will not help you find a solution. If you think you have only two choices, then you'll have a dilemma. If you can expand your viewpoint and come up with three or more choices, then you will be empowered to make a better decision.

8. Make your decision and move forward.

PART 3:
REFOCUS

CHAPTER NINE:
THE SUPER STRENGTH OF INTUITION

I'M NOT A doctor. I hold no medical or scientific degrees, only an honorary bachelor's degree that I was awarded decades after my school days. But I can tell you this: Your gut bone is connected to your head bone.

Intuition is a superpower that you can trust if you put in the time to develop it through critical thinking. You can train your intuition — your gut — to be a trustworthy advisor.

I've learned to listen to what my gut tells me over the years. It has developed a high level of sense through regular exercise and experience. My strategy is to gather as much information as I can and then let my brain and gut duke it out. My gut is virtually undefeated. Every time that I feel a strong intuition and follow it, I am happy that I did.

In 1980, I packed all my belongings into a 1966 Chevelle and small trailer and headed south from Minneapolis. The plan was to move to Colorado Springs, Colorado, to be a resident athlete at the Olympic Training Center for speed skating. It was a hastily thrown-together trip decided on only two weeks before. But it felt right at the time. I was ready for a new challenge, environment, and experience. I listened to my gut and threw myself headfirst into the unknown.

A friend of mine and fellow speed skater, John Debolt, joined me. We drove straight through to Kansas City, where we stopped for the night. In the morning, our plans changed.

"Hey, I know a girl in Wichita," John said. "We don't have to be in Colorado for three more weeks. Let's go down and visit her. It will be fun."

My brained shrugged. My gut said, "Hell, yeah!"

Three weeks later, John decided to marry the girl and stay in Wichita.

Stupid gut. Now I was faced with a new slate of decisions. I was running out of money and had to decide whether to continue to Colorado on my own, go back to Minneapolis, or stay in Wichita. I would let my head decide this time.

Here is what my head said.

"Ford, if you opened a map of the United States in search of a place to live, would you land on Wichita, Kansas? Come on, man. Be reasonable. You know you wouldn't."

Head was right. I wouldn't. But I wasn't ready to go back home. For one, that would feel like a failure, and secondly, I was ready for a new life far away from there. But was I really ready to train for the Olympics, for the many months of sweat and sacrifice with no sure reward at the end other than to be among several other amateur hopefuls? And did I want to go through all those trials alone in a strange new place without my friend, John, or anyone else that I knew? I checked with my heart. "Nope, nope," it said. "Lub-dub. Lub-dub."

Ok, stupid gut. What've you got?

"Ford," it said. "I've got a good feeling about this place."

My gut was right, and I haven't questioned it since. Wichita has been my happy, productive, and profitable home for over 35 years. Every time I was homesick for friends in Minneapolis or tempted to move to the east or west coasts, I was compelled to stay. I credit it to my trusty intuition. Seems like every time I would consider leaving, within a day or week I would get some amazing new opportunity. My gut was right, and I haven't questioned it since.

Over the years, I've learned to quiet my mind and listen to my intuition. My instinct and intuition have served me well in many areas of my life.

THE POWER TO PAUSE

Do you listen to your intuition regularly, or do you doubt your instincts? Often you hear people say, "I just have this gut feeling" or "I need to follow my heart." Regardless of what everyone else is telling them, they are firm in their beliefs and desire to move forward with whatever it is they are passionate about. How often do you listen to your heart or your gut to help you make wise decisions? How often has someone swayed you from following your instinct or intuition—and how has that worked out for you?

Are you using your instinct and intuition superpowers? Or are you letting other people influence and change your decisions based on fear, not facts? I am not a fan of organized religion, but I certainly am very spiritual. I certainly do believe in a higher power. Consider that old saying: "Let go, let God." How often do you let go and listen to what your instinct and intuition tell you? Les Brown used to say, "Leap, and grow your wings on the way down." Move forward in faith, and as you get new information, you always have the choice to change your mind or reevaluate to make a wiser, more educated decision.

CHAPTER 9 KEY CONCEPTS:

- Trust your gut
- Hone your business intuition

ACTION STEPS:

Let's Explore Tuning in to Your Inner Guidance

1. **Be a continual learner.** The fact that you're reading this book and exploring new ways to improve your performance and results validates that you're interested in learning.

2. **Look back** over your life and consider how well you listened to your instincts and intuition.

3. **Quiet your mind.** Take moments each day to clear your mind of distractions. I like to practice meditation. Find solitude where you can be in a quiet place without any interruptions. Put down your phone, turn off the computer, radio, and TV, and find solitude with yourself.

4. **Practice being the observer.** Stepping back from the situation will give you new perspectives and allow your intuition to assist you.

5. **Follow your hunches.** You will be amazed at the results you get.

6. **Exercise your intuition.** Your instincts are like muscles. The more you exercise them, the stronger they become and the more you can do with them.

CHAPTER TEN:
SUPERHUMAN SIMPLICITY

Do you sometimes wonder why other people achieve monumental success...and you're working just as hard and are coming up with ideas that are just as good, but you're still struggling? Or have you ever seen some crazy product on an infomercial and said to yourself, "Hey, I thought of that!" Yet you're not the one collecting millions of dollars from the sale of that product. Those are clues that you need to look more closely at your process. Some of this may boil down to the difference between the can't-do and can-do attitudes. But some of the problems may also be in the strategies you are using to get where you want to go.

I constantly run across situations where people make life way too hard for themselves.

Are you the type of person — or do you work for an organization — that seems to have too many levels of complexity, processes, or procedures? Let me be clear: I believe in creating processes and procedures to improve performance and produce consistent results. However, I encourage you to evaluate your strategies, tactics, and performance results from time to time and ask yourself if there is an easier, simpler, or better way. Ask yourself, "Am I making this too difficult? Are there steps that I could eliminate or avoid and achieve the same or better results?"

I think it's interesting how many times in my life the answers to problems were right in front of me, yet because I felt that it certainly couldn't be that easy, it wasn't. I see this with the clients I work with regularly. To help set the stage for a story, I need to give you some background. My target markets are organizations that want to find, attract, and keep their customers. This includes franchise brands, corporations, entrepreneurs, and associations.

Corporations hire me to grow their business, and associations hire me to add value to their membership. This is common for business owners looking for strategies to increase sales and profits. Since I am a professional keynote speaker, author, and consultant on business growth, marketing, and leadership, I have attracted many other top thought-leaders, speakers, authors, and consultants as clients. They love to work with my creative agency, Prime Concepts Group, because we understand their business model. We have vast experience in creating value propositions from intellectual how-to information.

ENJOY THE RIDE

Staples' office supplies stores had a moment of advertising brilliance when they branded around the concept "that was easy." I liked it so much that I ordered Easy Buttons™ for our offices. If you feel like the process is too hard, what will make it easier? Put on your critical thinking cap and make a list of ideas to explore. There are no wrong answers here, hopefully just a realization that life doesn't have to be complicated. You have the power to choose. Pick the hard way or tap on your mental "I'm making this easy" button.

CHAPTER TEN: SUPERHUMAN SIMPLICITY

Are you the type of person who wants to make every day too hard? Does your life seem like one long series of problems filled with struggles and heartache? Imagine what your life will be like when you adopt the superpower practices of this book, learn to let go, and unleash your inner brilliance.

CHAPTER 10 KEY CONCEPTS:

- Keep it simple
- Enjoy the ride

ACTION STEPS:

Making Your Life Easier

1. List three things in your life that you feel are too complicated.

2. Write a few sentences describing your thoughts and observations related to each topic that you think is too complicated.

3. Ask yourself what steps could be eliminated that would allow you to reach the same result.

4. Practice making your life easier by cleaning out the clutter in your life, getting enough sleep, exercising, eating nourishing foods, taking care of yourself first, and not trying to please everybody else.

5. Be curious about life, and don't be scared to gain new knowledge or to let go of old ideas.

CHAPTER TEN: SUPERHUMAN SIMPLICITY

6. Don't take yourself too seriously, have the capacity to laugh at yourself, and turn failure into fascination.

7. Focus on being productive, not just being busy. Don't mistake movement for productivity.

8. Learn to accept change as an integral part of life, as change is inevitable.

9. Don't wait for the situation to be perfect. Work with what you have, where you are now in your life, and take action toward achieving your goals.

CHAPTER ELEVEN:
THE POWER OF MONOTASKING

You still hear many people talking about how good they are at multitasking. What they're good at is deluding and distracting themselves. We are human beings, and human beings are built — whether they realize it or not — to do only one complicated task at a time. That's just how we're wired. We make ourselves less effective and productive than we could be when we forget that.

This kind of distraction is a big problem today, and I think a lot of it connects to how we choose to use our tools. Don't get me wrong. I am a huge fan of technology when it's used properly. Sometimes, though, we use our technology in ways that just don't support us.

Are you really multitasking, or are you delusional about the number of tasks you're accomplishing and doing well?

MIND OVER MATTER

We are in a world right now where faster is associated with better. Many think that if you're not texting, typing, tweeting, reading, driving, eating, and streaming a show all at the same time, you're not getting things done. Or worse, you think you are missing out on important events. The truth is that you're much less effective when you're not totally focused on the task at hand.

Look at us: We've got iPads, we've got iPhones, we've got laptops, we've got GPS. We have amazing tools. All of this technology was supposed to make us more focused and more effective. Truth is, what it's done for many of us is give us what I call learned A.D.D.

What is that? It's the kind of attention-deficit disorder we train ourselves to take on. It gets worse and worse, making us less and less effective over time. But we think we're getting more done!

IS MULTITASKING WORTH DYING FOR?

One example of what I'm talking about is the epidemic of texting while driving. We taught ourselves to do that. When we have to put up billboards on the highways to remind us that we're not supposed to be writing notes to each other at the same time we're steering a two-ton piece of heavy equipment down a crowded interstate, then we know we've got a problem with learned A.D.D.

So, lesson number one is straightforward: Put the freaking phone down when you're driving. Your technology is not worth dying or killing someone for. As a cyclist, I've been almost run over dozens of times by distracted drivers. I don't know which is worse, drunk driving or driving while texting. What I do know is that you shouldn't do either one.

ONE THING AT A TIME

I repeat: We can do only one complicated task at a time if we expect to do it well. And we are delusional when we try to stack tasks on top of one another and call what we're doing multitasking.

So that means we're wasting more time and attention than we should by leaving our email open and jumping back and forth to check it every two minutes. We may think we're doing more work, but what we really need to do is block time out, turn off our notifications, turn off our phone, focus on one thing at a time, and get the quality of our attention as close to 100 percent as possible for an extended period. Then, when it's time, we need to move on to the next task and focus clearly on that.

STATUS ISSUES

Now, I know that many people will push back against what I'm saying here because they're in love with this idea of themselves as being more efficient when they zip back and forth at one hundred miles an hour. They've built that myth of multitasking right into their self-image and professional identity. For a lot of people, it's a status issue. The more screens they have open at the same time, the more they imagine they're doing simultaneously with their technology, the more important they feel, and the more valuable they think they are to their organization.

That's a myth. Look around, and you'll see that the people who are most valuable to any organization are the people who have trained themselves to focus on one task at a time. If you really want to enhance your status in the organization, do what they're doing — one thing at a time.

And you know what? The people who make phones and tablets and laptop computers and so on haven't really challenged that myth that multitasking equals status. Why? Because the myth helps them sell more of their equipment.

I'm all for selling cool tools, tools that do what they're supposed to do, but sometimes I think we need to make more distinctions about what is productive and what is distracting.

ZIPPING IN AND OUT OF PARKING SPACES

Some people can think fast, jump from one topic to another, and then repeat the process. Some people have strengths that go in other directions. Shouldn't we play to our strengths? Absolutely. But at the same time, we don't want to kid ourselves about how much we're getting done or how we're spending our personal resources. As Jim Taylor suggests, we have to get a little clearer about how much gas we're really burning, how often we're slamming on the brakes, and where we're actually going.

We can choose to zip in and out of 30 different parking spaces in the same parking lot for half an hour, but we need to ask ourselves: Are we getting as far in that half-hour, but as we would if we pulled out of one parking space and then spent 30 minutes driving, with full, focused attention, to the next destination on our list? Then, when we pulled into the next parking space, we would have gotten somewhere. We would have accomplished one task within that half-hour.

DON'T DING!

I once had someone in my office who would leave his phone on all day long. And every single time he got an email, his phone dinged.

No matter what he was working on, as soon as that phone dinged, he'd pick it up and look at it. Well, the distraction and the lack of focus were costing him literally hours of productivity every day. But he had deluded himself into believing he was more efficient by doing what he was doing.

After auditing his time on projects, I saw he was more than 50 percent slower on tasks than the other team members. I tried to coach him to improve and turn his phone off, yet he just didn't want to do it. In the end, I gave him an opportunity for new career development elsewhere. I fired him.

Now I tell people in my office: Turn off your notifications, and you will get more done. My motto is "one thing at a time ... to 100 percent."

Schedule specific times to check your email during the day, and don't break that schedule. You'll find that life won't end if you're not constantly interrupted by your email.

Follow this one simple idea, and you'll improve your productivity. Set your phone on vibrate, and tell people to call you, rather than email or text you, when they have a true emergency. Then focus on one task at a time.

MANAGING INTERRUPTIONS

How do you expect to get any work done if you are constantly interrupted? Interruptions come from more than just texting, calls, and emails. What about your work environment? Are you constantly interrupted by your coworkers? Now, as we discuss interruptions, I want to clarify that I'm not talking about customer inquiries or essential communications. I'm referring more to managing your interruptions. Everyone in my office knows that a sales inquiry deserves immediate attention and is not an interruption. When our phones ring, we have a receptionist and specific call groups to route the calls. However, we have scheduled time blocked for reviewing and responding to emails.

I've always prided myself at Prime Concepts for having an open-door policy. For years, I encouraged my employees to come to me whenever they had a question or concern. The problem was that I didn't set any boundaries or guidelines initially. Now, each one of them has a spiral notebook titled "Ford list." Here's how it works. During the day, they capture items they need to discuss with me in the notebook, and then I have specific block times when we meet to cover their questions. We use the ABC method: *A* means absolutely necessary, *B* means they need an answer or resolution before a specific date, and *C* means they can wait. This helps them prioritize their needs and has markedly improved the performance and productivity of our team.

As an innovative thinker programmed to make processes and performance better, I sometimes get off track and go into training mode with my staff. For example, a team member came to me to review a 65-page document of website copy for one of our clients and just needed my review and approval. As I reviewed the content, other ideas came to me about how she could find out more about keyword research and integrating specific keyword phrases to help web pages rank higher in the search engines. She recognized that I was going to get off track, and since she's been trained in how to manage interruptions also, we moved that training task to the parking lot. The parking lot is a place to capture ideas and thoughts that we don't want to forget but don't necessarily need to be taken care of at that moment. I have a large whiteboard in my office for a parking lot and one in our conference room. Using the ABC method, blocking time, and parking topics for later has given us many more productive hours each week.

STAYING FOCUSED IS A SUPERPOWER

I can tell you that since I first noticed the learned A.D.D pattern, I've gone in the direction of only using one tool at a time, with one window open at a time, to work toward attaining one goal at a time. And I can tell you without any doubt that I am getting much more done, faster, and producing much better results.

CHAPTER 11 KEY CONCEPTS:

- One task at a time
- Manage your interruptions
- Stay focused

ACTION STEPS:

Ask yourself:

1. How much of the time and energy available to me am I wasting each day by jumping between tasks?

2. How many years have I been conditioning myself, after years of using computers, to have multiple windows open at the same time and to jump between windows?

3. How well is that way of working serving me? Does it play to my strengths? What would happen if I tried working in a different way for one straight day and compared the results?

PART 4:
REIGNITE

CHAPTER TWELVE:
UP, UP AND AWAY

You picked up this book and have read this far for a reason — you're on a mission. You have ambition. You have dreams. You have goals you want to achieve in your life, leadership, or business. That's great! Now, let's get leverage. A mighty action plan (MAP) can help you gain momentum and make it all happen.

Your MAP consists of clearly laid out steps to achieve your clear vision for success.

How big is your goal? Do you want to lose 10 pounds, become a best-selling author, transform your business from a mom-&-pop to a corporate dynasty? Or perhaps you're the CEO of a Fortune 500 company and want to see sales increase over the next five years by at least 20 percent a year.

You have a goal, a target market (or multiple markets) you want to reach, and now you need a plan.

My favorite way to get started on an action plan is to use mind mapping. This can give you a one-page snapshot of all the moving parts and pieces needed to execute your plan.

Whether you decide to use a mind map or follow some other format, you must create the initial plan, a brain dump of everything you think you want to do. No one else can do that for you.

The next step is to categorize those different ideas into no more than five or six sections and then prioritize the outcomes you want. You should become very outcome-focused, not task-focused. What do you need to do? What does success look like? What do you need to do to get that outcome? What are you willing to do that's lifestyle-friendly? That term *lifestyle-friendly* means, for example, that I can tell you how to lose weight, but if following those steps are not lifestyle-friendly to you, you're not going to do it.

It's all about selecting the activities congruent with what you're willing to do and your goals. Your motivation comes from the level of pain you have that you want to make go away or from the specific desire or pleasure you want to achieve. What we've always done in my business when it comes to launching a new product line includes writing a mighty action marketing plan first. We determine the outcomes, specific strategies, milestones, and timelines. Every website project we develop, every digital marketing campaign or social media campaign, starts with deciding the desired outcomes. We plan around those outcomes and define and use predetermined metrics to measure them.

THE MAP IN ACTION

You can create a MAP for virtually any goal or outcome you want in your personal or professional life. For example, a client came to us who would be speaking to a new group in a few weeks, but she didn't have any specific products they could purchase after her presentation to help them continue their learning journey. She knew, though, that she could help them continue to make improvements even after her presentation. Together, we used the MAP process to help her build and visualize the plan for the new product she could offer to that audience.

CHAPTER TWELVE: UP, UP AND AWAY

I called the meeting planner and asked her to give me details about the group and the presenters they had hired in the past. She described a group of pharmacy owners and pharmacists who typically spend only a couple of hundred dollars attending her events. She mentioned that they were very conservative, so if we were going to offer them information product resources, like an audio program, it couldn't cost over $197. I asked her for a few names of the pharmacists who would be attending the event in Florida. She emailed me links to their websites and their contact information.

I interviewed a few people planning to attend the conference and discovered that they were interested in transforming the culture of their workplaces and growing their businesses. My client, a workplace culture expert, specialized in business transformations, so I went through the action planning process to outline the new video training product and the strategy to sell it. She didn't have the video content yet, but she said she would present on the topic area.

She had only a couple of weeks before she had to give her presentation. There was virtually no time to develop the content, shoot and edit it, or design the packaging of the physical product. Here's what we did: My team designed a small tabletop display and promotional flyers with a mock picture of the product, title, sales copy, and order forms that we would distribute during her presentation. With an investment of under $500, we were set.

I called the client back and told her the complete concept and outline.

"It sells for $997," I said.

"You mean $97," she replied.

I assured her that I had not misspoken.

"That won't work," she said. "It's too expensive. The meeting planner said they typically only spend a couple of hundred bucks."

I insisted.

"We've got a good plan. Let's work with it, and let the market tell us what works."

"But we don't have a product," she said.

"Don't worry about the product. Take the signs and order forms to the event. If you don't sell any videos, don't worry. We won't produce it. But if you take it and sell it, then we will produce the new product, and it will be well worth the effort."

The plan was set. She flies to Florida to present to the pharmacy group. Three-quarters of the way through her presentation, she mentions, "If you like what you've heard here and you want to continue the journey, come see me. I have a special resource that can help you implement many of the concepts we've covered today when you get back to your organization."

She called me from the airport later.

"Oh, I love you, I love you, I love you," she said. "We just sold 95 packages at $997."

That was over $90,000 of product sales from an audience of only 400 people the meeting planner thought would never invest that kind of money on resources. This experience isn't an exception. I've found that so-called experts often give poor advice not backed up by experience or real numbers, and those limiting beliefs put restrictions on what's possible.

Now, she still had to produce the product, but with $90,000 in orders, she could certainly afford to spend a couple of days in the studio shooting the footage. Keep in mind that she had all the valuable content. All she had to do was say it on camera. What we did was leverage her intellectual property and create a new value proposition...because of the MAP.

PICTURE PROSPERITY

If you're someone who hasn't started a company yet but wants to get your personal or professional life on track, your mapping process would start by creating a prosperity dream board, a.k.a. a vision board and getting really clear on what you want to DO, HAVE, or BECOME.

What are the areas of your life that are most imto you right now?

Here are a few categories to get your creative juices flowing:

- ▶ Goals
- ▶ Family
- ▶ Career
- ▶ Friends
- ▶ Animals
- ▶ Volunteering/Community
- ▶ Home
- ▶ Hobbies
- ▶ Self-care
- ▶ Money
- ▶ Health/Wellness (Physical and Mental)
- ▶ Travel
- ▶ Romantic Relationships
- ▶ Values
- ▶ Growth Opportunities

Get out some scissors and glue and make a poster. Sounds silly, but I'm serious. You must create a clear picture in your mind of what you want and then put it on paper. You can't do the plan without the outcome.

Post the dream board somewhere you can see it every day. Seeing the images frequently will program them into your subconscious mind. This creates a desire to take the daily action steps that bring your dreams closer to reality.

Start collecting magazines, brochures, images from the internet, and other materials in the hobbies and areas you are interested in. Divide your map into sections such as work, spiritual, relationships, wealth, fun, and fitness. There are no rules for how you put items on the prosperity map, except that the image must be meaningful to you. It doesn't matter if anyone else understands it. It's not for them.

Once you have the outcomes captured, put the strategies and tactics of the plan in writing. Think on paper, not in your head. Create your capture list, categorize the items into sections and subsections, and estimate what resources you'll need and the timelines. This sounds elementary, but you'd be surprised how many people complain about their poor results, yet they don't have a written plan of attack or take action to improve their situation.

Create your written plan, but make sure you have a set of measurements in place to check and see if you're on track so that you can make the necessary course corrections. Then the key is to be able to work the plan and use your feedback and metrics to determine whether the plan is working.

NO SKIPPING AHEAD

I want to encourage you not to skip this step. You might be thinking, "Oh, I know all this." Then where is your dream board? Where is your prosperity board? Do you have it on your computer? Do you have pictures of what you want to do, have, or become? Is it on a screen saver? Do you have it on your phone? Is it printed out? Do you really have a truly clear idea of what you want in the different roles of your life?

Use these tools to get clear about your unique answer to the question: How do you want to live your life?

Remember, this isn't about acquiring stuff. It is about becoming. You might achieve serenity, become a great parent, or give back to your community or a philanthropic cause. My point is that I truly believe that the purpose of life is to be a developing human spirit and to do that you need to be continually learning. That's what I want this book to help you with, to give you insights on how to unleash your inner superpowers to improve the quality of your life and the lives of those around you.

Back to the dream board. There should be images you can see that brings your success into existence before you start executing the plan. I apply it to my life. For example, before I wrote this book, I made a mock-up cover design and hung it in my office. Before even submitting the book proposal to the publisher, I designed a book cover and media release. Before I was successful in business, I wrote headlines about myself and visualized them appearing in my favorite business magazine.

YOUR X-RAY VISION SUPERPOWER

A few years ago, I was hired to present to Global Spectrum, a subsidiary of Comcast. The company hosts a wide array of popular sports and entertainment events, trade shows, performing arts, and other special events. I was first hired to present to Global Spectrum's area general managers and sales and marketing teams. Their offices are in Philadelphia, and I found out they worked closely with the Philadelphia Flyers of the National Hockey League, the 76ers National Basketball Association team, and some farm league teams for hockey and baseball. When I returned home, I thought how cool it would be to provide marketing insights for an NBA and NHL team.

Soon after thinking about them and adding their logos to my prosperity manifestation map, I received a call from Global Spectrum and the teams' marketing managers to prepare and present customized training for the Flyers and 76ers group ticket sales teams. I was flown to Philly a couple of times and attended a Flyers hockey game and a 76ers basketball game as a VIP. Do I think that adding their logos to my dream board was some hocus-pocus? No, but I do believe that I attracted that opportunity into my life through focused effort and my MAP. Not to get too magical, but I do believe that we attract objects, people, and situations into our lives that we focus on. If you're mainly tuned into a negative channel of thought, I can guarantee that you'll manifest pain and negativity into your life. Through visualization and an action plan, you can transform your life.

This pattern has played out for all the significant accomplishments I've had in my life. When I projected it, my mind went there first, and then my body and the world worked to manifest it.

You can do a simple sketch. It doesn't have to be fancy or cost a lot of money. You just need a clear vision of why you want what you want, and make sure it's congruent with all the specific actions in your life — because you can't have two conflicting goals and expect to get to your destination. You also can't just dream about it; you have to get off your butt and take action. The key is to have a plan, so you aim your efforts in the right direction.

Taking the time to create your mighty momentum action plan is one of the most critical steps to your success. With your plan in place, you will be super powerful, confident, and ready to move forward toward your goals.

In fact, *action* is a superpower. Being able to take action and execute the steps in your plan is what will make the difference between a life of quiet desperation and one of health, wealth, and fulfillment.

CHAPTER 12 KEY CONCEPTS:

- MAP your goals
- Get really clear on what you want to DO, HAVE, or BECOME
- Create your vision board

ACTION STEPS:

Are you ready to create, visualize, and take action on your plan? Good. Get started!

1. Have you created your Vision/Dream Board yet? (YES/NO)

2. Have you made your brain dump capture list? (YES/NO)

3. Have you sorted and categorized items based on your roles, goals, and dreams? (YES/NO)

4. Have you created your massive momentum action plan? (YES/NO)

CHAPTER THIRTEEN:
BULLETPROOF TIME MANAGEMENT

So, you have a MAP. Now what? You need strategies and tactics to move forward and gain momentum.

That's what this next part of the book is all about. If you have made it this far, you are ready to be personally accountable for taking action on your own plan. You are not part of the vast majority of the herd who sit on the sidelines and comment on what other people do out there in the game of life. You are ready to take the field and run a play. Once you become one of those people — the people who regularly take action on their behalf, the people who get leverage on themselves — you have joined a pretty exclusive league of superheroes. You have become someone who takes responsibility for your own outcomes.

SIMPLE VS. EASY

It's simple to do what we know we need to do to move forward toward achieving our goals. For example, the strategy for losing weight is simple. Cut down on the calories you consume, exercise more so you burn the calories, or do both. The process is simple...but it's not necessarily easy. If it were, we'd all look like supermodels with the body of our dreams.

The same goes for the business sector. The strategy to make money in business is simple. Really, when you get right down to it, there are only four possible ways to generate more income for your business. They are:

1. **Get more customers.** Not more, but more high-value customers.

2. **Increase the frequency of purchases.** Encouraging repeat and referral sales.

3. **Increase the average transaction value.** Get them to spend more with you.

4. **Lower your operating expenses.** Improve your operational efficiencies.

And that's it. That's all there is to it. End of business class, right? Well, no. Like the weight loss example, the strategy that works may be simple enough, but executing it is not easy in practice. This is where it becomes essential to identify what you're not great at and then find resources that can leverage your time. It's an important self-management tactic. You're looking for a way to get the best results with less effort. How do we get that done? There are three steps:

1. Understand your core competencies.
2. Buckle down and do the work.
3. Delegate the work to someone skilled and competent.

And when it comes to delegation, that process is done most effectively after you've deleted all the distractions and figured out what *you* have to do; then, you can really know what to delegate and outsource. Ask yourself: "What better use could I make of my time?" I have someone who cleans our house, someone who cleans our pool, and someone who mows our lawn. Why? Because I delegated those responsibilities. Ask yourself, "Is the majority of my time spent on the highest and best use of my time?" This will help you uncover opportunities to leverage your time and hire your weaknesses.

That's a big step in leveraging your success and making progress on the stuff that looks simple but isn't easy: using delegation strategies.

PLAY TO YOUR STRENGTHS

For you, getting leverage might mean finding a partner or outsourcing: finding someone who can do their core competency better than you can and then paying them to do it for you. Even though we have a team of competent professionals on staff at Prime Concepts Group, we utilize virtual assistants and outsource specific tasks. With the advances in technology, especially video conferencing and cloud computing, it's easier than ever to utilize talent around the globe. The covid pandemic created many new firms that specialize in providing remote workers. While there are many, we've found great candidates on Upwork.com.

Knowing what your core competencies are is essential. It means knowing what your fastball is. You need to know where your strength lies and spend most of your time and energy, your wattage, and your power on that. In business, I believe people are good at one of these three areas: *marketing* (selling a product), *management* (operations), or *production* (manufacturing a product or providing a service). At best, you may be competent in two of the three, but rarely are you strong in all three areas.

For example, I understand management and operations, but my strengths are in marketing and delivering innovative marketing and sales campaigns. If you're in business or in business leadership, you need to have a broad spectrum of knowledge, including your brands, products, services, industry, value propositions, and competitive advantages, but to be effective, you need to leverage your strengths.

I'm not a big believer in strengthening your weaknesses. You should learn from and grow out of your weaknesses, but you need to focus most of your time on your core strengths. Getting into the habit of playing to your strengths is another idea that sounds simple but isn't easy. It's like building muscle. You have to do it over and over again until it becomes second nature.

At the end of the day, I believe the first and most important step when it comes to getting leverage on yourself is not to make the mistake of thinking that because it is simple — because you understand it — taking action is easy. Until you've practiced using your superpowers, taking action on your goals may not be easy. It takes work, it takes persistence, and it takes deciding to get back up after being knocked down. You just need to decide to settle in and do the work you love, delegate the work you don't, and then take steps that support you. What's the alternative? Really, there's only one: setting up and reinforcing a habit of avoidance. You know the kind of habit I'm talking about: We set aside time on our calendar specifically to make forward progress on our goal, we're just about to take action...and suddenly we decide that it's really, really important to start vacuuming the rug. Or clean out the refrigerator. Or to check our email, Facebook, and LinkedIn pages.

This is what's called *approach-avoidance*. It means steering clear of what you're supposed to do. You must delete the distractions and either do the work or delegate the work.

That's what I mean by getting leverage. Don't let distractions be an excuse for not getting done what you need to get done.

TAKE CONTROL OF YOUR DAY

To plan your day and prioritize your tasks, you should know how to say no to nonessential tasks and break down larger tasks into smaller categories and more manageable tasks. Just the effort of putting ideas into categories in chunk sizes reduces your stress and keeps you more productive. It's a method of evaluating how you're spending your time.

Keeping a journal — like your Hero Handbook — is one of the first and most important steps of good time management. This one tool will help you lose weight, close sales, or do whatever else you need to do. When I consult with salespeople, I have them time themselves with a stopwatch while they're on the phone selling or face-to-face with a client. At the end of the day, I have them add up how much time they spent actually selling... face-to-face or in 2-way conversations. Most of the time it ends up being less than an hour a day. The rest of their time is taken up by extraneous activities that they thought contributed to selling but weren't as important as communicating with prospects and clients. The same analogy works with marketing — you must limit your distractions and block out your time effectively. That means getting plenty of sleep, dieting, and exercising. You have to make sure that you're healthy, and there are plenty of resources available to help you do that.

THE POWER TO SAY NO

Many people talk themselves into believing that they are productive when they're not. They're just busy. We need to stay away from that delusion. Often, the best way to meet this challenge is to find an accountability partner to keep you on task and accountable by discussing your actual allocations of time during the day.

You're on track, and it's time to execute. Now the question is how the work that needs to happen gets done. Do you have the skills and talent to do it all yourself? Who on your team can you delegate tasks to so your projects and goals can move forward? Have you established a realistic timeline for accountability?

Time management is a superpower. Be more than busy. Be productive. Be effective. Take action on your goal.

CHAPTER 13 KEY CONCEPTS:

- Understand your strengths
- Take action
- Delegate

ACTION STEPS:

Over the past week, how many times did you...

1. ... say "no" to nonessential tasks? _____

2. ... break down larger tasks into smaller categories and more manageable to-do items? _____

CHAPTER 10 KEY CONCEPTS

CHAPTER FOURTEEN:
MENTORSHIP MAGIC

Superman and Jor-El. Spiderman and Uncle Ben. Luke Skywalker and Obi-Wan Kenobi. Just about every great superhero has a mentor. Mentors are the key to unlocking our superpowers. Once you have the right mentor, you have a special kind of role model: someone whose example helps you when you need guidance most, someone who makes it easier for you to learn and grow from your weaknesses, someone who can help you maximize your strengths and get the help you need in the areas where you lack expertise.

Most people don't realize it, but there are three different kinds of mentors. Once you know how to take full advantage of all three kinds of mentor relationships, you will have access to new levels of power, influence, self-confidence, and authority that most other people only dream about. You become a different kind of person: the strongest possible version of you. It's almost like magic. In fact, from a distance, the quantum leap you will take in your life will look so much like magic that that transformation might as well *be* magic.

The magic of mentorship emerges from three very different sources:
1. A coach who challenges you helps you set goals and holds you accountable for getting the most from your own talents and abilities.

2. A mastermind group.

3. Someone who is not personally known to you, but who serves as an important role model, and whose life, career, and decisions you study closely. (This person may be alive or dead.) We call these people Legacy Masters. Let's look closely at each of these three groups now, but first a word of caution.

We live in an age where anyone with a webcam can claim to be a mentor or life coach. Before you hire a mentor, make sure that person has accomplishments in life that align with your goals. Beware of the impostors that offer get-rich, get-fit, get- (fill in the blank) quick schemes. Just use your common sense and have your B.S. detector turned up too high.

MENTOR GROUP ONE: COACHES

When it comes to getting a professional coach, the purpose for you is twofold. You've got personal, one-on-one accountability, as well as identifying a leader for you. In my professional life, I've hired coaches for accountability training, business growth, and leadership expertise.

This kind of mentor can offer advice and help hold you personally accountable for making the changes you need to make. The most popular example of this kind of mentor is the entrepreneur or executive who takes a promising young newcomer on as a protégé. Andrew Carnegie, for instance, was a mentor to Charles M. Schwab, the first president of U.S. Steel. One of my favorite books is *The Compound Effect* by Darren Hardy, the publisher of Success Magazine. He credits many of his success strategies to his mentors, like Jim Rohn and others.

You can also work with a whole different kind of coach, someone who has a skill or ability that you don't. Here, the mentor is not so much helping you grow as filling a gap for you. Although there is still the potential for you to learn from the relationship, both you and the mentor expect the mentor to act on your behalf — and do stuff you aren't in a position to do.

Whether you choose a professional coach or an expert in a certain area of expertise, you want someone who's going to tell you the truth, someone who's not judgmental, someone who's a critical thinker and willing to call it tight. You want someone who will challenge your assumptions and help you spot your own BS. I have had several great individual mentors, the legendary author, educator, and multi-millionaire Nido Qubein being one. Each mentor is in my life for a different reason, fulfilling a different role, but all have helped me unleash and develop my potential. It's an ongoing journey.

A common mistake people make with coaches is to assume that it is the coach's responsibility to ensure that you achieve your goal. It's not. It's yours. You're responsible for your actions or lack of actions.

MENTOR GROUP TWO: MASTERMIND GROUPS

For my business, I prefer to work with accountability masters who help hold *each other* accountable. This is a common variation in this mentor relationship, commonly known as a mastermind group. A mastermind group allows participants to both lead and follow, to act as both mentor and mentee, depending on their skill set and the situation they face.

I've been a member of many mastermind groups over the years, and I've created my own inner circle mastermind groups. These are programs that people invest up to $25,000 in and must meet certain conditions to be a member. Want to know why? Because people will pay large sums of money to get great ideas and solutions to their problems and then be held accountable for implementing them. That's really the essence of entering into this kind of mentor relationship: getting ideas and being held personally accountable for what you know you need to do next.

The feeling of a good mastermind group that creates very close relationships and very high levels of achievement is hard to compare. For example, I take part in a mastermind group made up of some of the nation's top professional speakers, called a Speakers Roundtable. It's composed of 20 elite and successful speakers in America. (You can learn more about them at SpeakersRoundtable.com.) We get together twice a year in person and also have monthly virtual meetings and updates to work on our business and personal initiatives. It's a very tight group and hard to get invited to participate in. What makes it work as well as it does is the power of peer pressure and the depth of experience of the members. You really don't want to show up for one of those meetings, or dial into one of those zoom meetings, without having taken the actions that you told the group you were going to take!

I'm also part of a mastermind group organized through EO, the Entrepreneurs Organization (eonetwork.org). This particular group gets together once a month in what's called an E.O. forum session, where six to 12 of us go over business and personal issues. It's noncompetitive, confidential, and very tight. Confidentiality and rapport are necessary because entrepreneurs often don't get the opportunity for unbiased feedback from the people they work with. Business owners can't just confide in their employees and bring problems home to their spouses or other family members as that usually creates conflict or varied advice. So, this type of mastermind group is an invaluable tool and one of the big reasons I really believe in the concept of the mastermind. When these groups are put together properly, they can be extremely powerful.

What you have to avoid, though, is a competitive group, where people are trying to show each other up or score points on each other. In those cases, people are hesitant to talk about what they do because they are afraid their competition will capitalize on a unique idea they come up with. These groups can fail when they're not made up of prosperity-minded individuals who are truly interested in hearing constructive criticism and letting the group serve as a collective accountability master. When egos get in the way, and judging happens, the group falls apart. You also need to watch out for cases when one person starts to dominate the group, either with their own rules or needs. Bottomline.

The key for success is to have a mastermind group that's not too big and not too small — between three and 10 is a good target — and is made up of diverse individuals who are all critical thinkers interested in getting good feedback. I mean feedback that will help them grow, personally and professionally. Members must be givers, not takers, and respect each other's confidentiality.

One more thing: To enjoy the benefits of having an accountability master within one of these groups, you must be willing to be somebody else's accountability master. You have to be sincerely interested in the success of the other person. You have to be a giver, not just a taker.

MENTOR GROUP THREE: LEGACY MASTERS

This is what happens when you choose to study and model the best practices of mentors you don't know personally. Once you have decided on your role, and you know exactly what it is you want to achieve, you find people who have done it already, you ignore the fact that you don't know them, and you learn as much as you can, so you can model their example.

Our technology and the internet make it possible to learn from mentors on YouTube, LinkedIn Learning, and other social media platforms. So no, you may not necessarily know your mentor on a personal level, but thanks to these resources, you can get direct instruction from them and discover an amazing amount about what they've done in their lives. That means you can learn new skills, master new lessons, adapt new ideas — and these can all help you improve. For example, if I wanted to model my leadership approach after Steve Jobs, using his life lessons and experiences, it's now possible for me to do that. This kind of mentor is key to unlocking our superpower.

The success I've accomplished in my own life has been based on legacy mentorship magic. When I was in a detention center as a young kid, someone gave me a cassette program of *The Strangest Secret,* narrated by Earl Nightingale. That audio cassette changed the course of my life. That was the first time I had ever heard positive programming, like "If you think that you can do it, you can; stop letting your past become an anchor that holds you back." That audio program started a long journey of personal and professional growth and development.

Soon after hearing that program, I started my first business. I let go of the past and started using the lessons I had gotten from that mentor, whom, of course, I had never met, never worked with, and never knew.

You need these types of people in your life, these great figures. They are the people who have scaled the heights and reached the top of the mountain. You need to learn what path they followed so you can follow it yourself.

There is power in the right relationships and having a mentor for personal or professional growth can be a vital asset in achieving your goals. Studies show that we are as successful as the people in our social circles. Who are the people you surround yourself with? Are they successful people? Do they have a positive, can-do attitude? Have they achieved the kind of success in life that you are striving for, and perhaps have insights that could help you along the way? Or are your closest friends always complaining, down on their luck, seeming to fail at whatever they do? The people you hang out with can make a huge difference in your ability to achieve success.

Why stay stuck in a rut or reinvent the wheel? Study successful people. Discover what makes them tick. What are their thought processes? How positive is their attitude about life? Find people you would like to emulate, be like, or befriend, and ask if they would be willing to be your mentor. Leverage your time, and spend time with positive, healthy, happy people who are on the ball and know how to use their superpowers to get things done. Emulate your mentors; show them that the valuable time they shared with you has not been wasted. Show them that you've used the tips and tools they have shared with you to achieve your own success.

Harness the power of the mastermind group — right now!

You now know about the importance of finding a mentor. I also encourage you to find or start a mastermind group just as soon as you possibly can. It might meet once a week, twice a month, or even once a month. You might meet for coffee at Starbucks, on a conference call, or a video chat.

Select a small number of people you feel will work well together and initiate your mastermind group. Several of my friends and business colleagues actively take part in multiple groups — each helps them target different areas of their personal and professional goals for continuous improvements.

CHAPTER 14 KEY CONCEPTS:

- Find a coach
- Create your Mastermind group
- Model your mentors

ACTION STEPS:

Creating a Mastermind Group

If you're on the search for a mentoring relationship, in your perfect world, who would you like to spend time with who could help you move farther, faster along your path? (Consider including "legacy" mentors like Steve Jobs or Napoleon Hill on this list.)

1. _____

2. _____

3. _____

4. _____

5. _____

Who would you like to mastermind with?

1. _____

2. _____

3. _____

4. _____

5. _____

CHAPTER FIFTEEN:
THE POWER OF GRATITUDE

When I joined EO, the Entrepreneurs' Organization (eonetwork.org), I went through an orientation to become part of the EO Forum. People talked to us about forum group rules, guidelines, and the benefits and procedures of the mastermind group. So that everyone could get acquainted with each other, they asked us to record a timeline of our lives and identify any crucial events that might have changed the course of our lives.

Then, they asked us to create a graph, starting from left to right. On the left would be where you were born, on the right would be the current day. They asked us to plot out events of our lives on a graph of positive and negative times in our lives. If the event was positive, it went up on the graph above the line, but if you had a negative experience, like getting cancer, for example, then you plotted below the neutral line. In other words, they tried to get a lifeline experience snapshot of the group members.

As we went around the table, my turn to share finally came, and I held up my sheet. My line was straight in a gradual positive progression. The group leader told me maybe I didn't understand the exercise, but my response was simple: I understood the exercise. I was appreciative and grateful for everything that had happened to me in my life.

Even though I grew up as a troubled teenager in foster care and detention centers, I was grateful for those experiences. I was a punk kid who carried a handgun, a terrible student, and just a generally reckless teen. I was an orphan, adopted, and I spent a lot of time running around on the streets. Now, I don't want to give you the wrong impression. I never missed a meal or shot anybody. But I was a misguided youth. Yet, I've found that now, looking back, those weren't actually negative times in my life *because I was learning all the time.* I was learning what I wanted and what I didn't want in my future.

So instead of labeling a specific moment in my life as positive or negative, I've been able to turn the perspective of the negatives in my life into positives...because I believe that life is a gift and holds appreciation and gratitude in my heart.

BRAVE AND BOLD

If you're allowing your fears and resentments about your past, your relationships, your career, or any other part of your life to hold you back, you need to take a step back. Evaluate what there is to be grateful about in that situation. What do you appreciate about that situation? Maybe you can appreciate that situation because it is a bad situation, and you now need to get out of it. And you need to change course. That's what they call a great leap forward. Make the choice; it's your life. That's worth being grateful for.

Now, I'm aware that some people may be coming to this book from the perspective of having been through major traumatic experiences in their past, like abuse, physical injury, or war. My message to you is that I am not a therapist: If you've got trauma that's dominating your life and taking you to a negative place on a regular basis, you need to look at what you have to do to change that. However, let me also point out that, once you've processed whatever it was that happened to you, you are still alive. You are above ground. You can choose to be grateful.

A lot of people die inside at 25. They're just not buried until they're 85 or older. They've given up on their talents, goals, and dreams.

The world moves along more efficiently when you show people a little love and appreciation. That means telling your mentors how much you appreciate their time and insights or thanking your team for helping you get it all done.

Once you've unleashed and developed superpowers, you'll find ways to benefit from virtually any situation, even a difficult situation. And you'll find you have a sense of gratitude and appreciation for whatever has come your way.

Harnessing gratitude and appreciation can be difficult, but it is essential to your emotional survival. Without denying whatever just happened to you, whether it seems positive or negative at the time, find some way to process it emotionally, learn from it, and, once you've mastered the lesson and come out on the other side, be genuinely *grateful* that it happened to you. That takes a little practice. But you can't be a true superhero without it.

Years ago, I was invited to train at the Olympic Training Center in Colorado Springs, Colorado. It was a speed skating camp for athletes who qualified. I trained there in 1984 and 1987, and while I didn't make the Olympic team, it was a fantastic experience. I could have easily just closed the book right there and said, "Well, I didn't make it. My life's over." But I didn't. You can't let one event close out your life early and become your entire entity. You are much more than a job title or role in your life. You are multifaceted and have many different roles. You can't let these events prevent you from seeing the world clearly. If trauma has happened in your life, you could draw whatever lessons from that experience to support you. Eventually, it's your choice.

It really is a mindset, and that is what this book is about. Allow yourself to use your superpower to transform what you think about what happened to your life and see what you can do to have appreciation and gratitude related to the experience.

I once had an employee who embezzled over $500,000 and stole truckloads of inventory from me. He oversaw my accounting and worked on some special projects for me. I found out that while I was out of town on a speaking engagement, he illegally entered my building; stole over $80,000 worth of inventory; got online and changed all our passwords to all our eCommerce servers; opened up another bank account, a shopping cart, and hosting account in his name; and attempted to open a competing business using our intellectual property and confidential resources!

Now, you might think that it would be hard to find reasons to be grateful in that situation. And you know what? You would be right. When I found out what had happened, I wasn't grateful at all. I was furious, and the incident led to more than a few sleepless nights.

The situation only seemed to get worse. This guy tried to take away one of my largest client accounts by convincing them to save commissions by working with him independently and paying a lower commission rate. I got even angrier. Yes, I am human.

Obviously, this could be categorized as a negative event. It was impacting my business to the tune of $675,000. I had to decide what to do. I decided to get past the anger, which I did, and then deal with the situation logically, positively. I filed a legal and civil court case for tortious interference. To help maintain my sanity, I set mental, emotional, and financial boundaries and expectations ahead of time.

Here's the point: I'm not at day one anymore, which means working hard to ensure that I'm not investing my time, energy, and life force in responsive anger and defense modes. I'm glad that this happened.

Read that part again. *I am glad that this happened.*

Why? Because it made me realize how lacking my oversight and accountability was in this person's position. I allowed this to happen by not putting the proper checks and balances in place to help prevent the situation. That was another life lesson. This guy didn't realize it, but he was doing important consulting work for my company. He taught me a lot about how to make sure this never, ever happens again.

He also gave me a great self-management lesson that I can share (and have shared) with many other people. One of the big reasons I'm writing this book is to help organizations make the most of the people they have: to keep their top employees, to get them to perform at higher levels without them quitting to work somewhere else. But when your organization hits bumps in the road, as mine did, that shouldn't take down your whole company. It's just not worth losing your company or your emotional balance over. You process it. You decide what happens next. Take corrective action. And then you move on.

Everyone gets life lesson tests…and you will keep getting these types of tests until you pass them. If you're serious about having a positive attitude, then when a situation like what happened to me happens to you, you won't spend weeks or days or months or years cursing at the person or the event. If that's your reaction, maybe your positive attitude isn't screwed on as tightly as it could be. I don't believe in ignoring a problem and acting like it didn't happen. I believe in working through the problem and moving on. Don't make it harder than it is or easier than it is; just see it for what it is.

Gratitude and appreciation are truly about not holding on to a problem once you've dealt with it emotionally and decided what to do about it. Let go. Take action...and be grateful for the lesson!

CHAPTER 15 KEY CONCEPTS:

- Be Brave and Bold
- Be grateful for the lesson
- Show your appreciation

ACTION STEPS:

Gratitude and appreciation are two more superpowers in your arsenal of tools to efficiently and effectively get things accomplished.

Who in your life are you most grateful for?

1. _____
2. _____
3. _____
4. _____
5. _____

Write these names in your Hero Handbook.

- What experiences in your life are you grateful for?
- Write them in your Hero Handbook.

- Who needs to be on your weekly list of people that you want to show appreciation to for being in your life?

List the names here and describe how you are going to show them appreciation.

1. _____

2. _____

3. _____

4. _____

5. _____

PART 5:
REFLECT

CHAPTER SIXTEEN:
THE POWER TO PIVOT

WHEN I STARTED Saeks Painting in 1976, I wanted to earn money differently than the other kids in the housing projects of North Minneapolis, Minnesota. I wanted to move from victimhood to a path where my decisions and actions had a positive effect on my life. I didn't understand words like prosperity, destiny, or success. The only things I understood were blame, poverty, fear of adults, fear of the police, fear of being alone, and frankly death.

After I was given the cassette tape, *The Strangest Secret* by Earl Nightingale, I heard a positive message for the first time in all my 15 years that changed the direction of my life. After that, when I would finish a painting job successfully and receive glowing remarks from the customer, it made me feel good about myself. I wanted that feeling over and over again, so I worked hard to please the customer.

I learned quickly that if *you* don't take care of the customer, somebody else will, and customers vote with their wallet. I had to develop the reflexes to learn from my mistakes and difficulties that I had faced. My business, and my life, helped me identify the need for loops and metrics of measurement to keep improving until I found success.

I understood the direct connection between my thoughts and my beliefs, how my beliefs determined my behavior and habits, how those habits influenced my actions, and how my actions (or inactions) determined my results. Whether you believe it or not, our world is directly affected by the decisions we make or fail to make.

I learned to take full control over the results in my life and started to understand that my actions lead to outcomes both good and bad. It's been proven many times throughout my personal and professional life.

POWERFUL PROGRESS

Let's take the concept covered in the previous chapter and build on it. So, you've got a mighty action plan in place, and you're moving forward to achieve your goals. **How are you going to know your plan is working?** Unfortunately, society has conditioned many of us to want instant gratification, and while success can come quickly, it rarely happens overnight. Anyone who achieved success probably spent many years developing the necessary skills and opportunities to reach their goals. The people I admire most failed quickly, sometimes more than once, then learned from their mistakes and picked themselves up to start again with more experience and insight. What do Henry Ford, Stan Lee, and George Foreman have in common? They all went bankrupt before they hit their stride in business!

When I am working on projects with my team at PCG, I like to do a premortem. This means looking at all the ways we might fail *before* we start, so we can limit the risks. As we execute, we want to have a feedback loop in place to measure success.

If you're not where you want be in any part of your life, start with what successful looks like for you. How are you going to measure it? What are you using as a reference for success? Are limiting beliefs holding you back, or are you willing to stretch yourself to get to the next level?

The reason I talk about mindset so much is because even with feedback loops and measurements, having critical thinking skills to be able to evaluate and draw conclusions that help you move forward are just as important as the tools you use to measure your progress.

Maybe you went through a divorce, lost a job, or a loved one passed away. While that may seem tragic in the moment, you're still responsible for how you perceive that event and what you do each day following that event.

For example, if you want to lose weight, there are apps to use on your phone for tracking and feedback, and all kinds of digital devices that track steps, heartrate, oxygen level, and optimal exercise zones to help you with your weight loss goals and measure your progress. The first step is knowing where you are, so you can determine where you're going.

ARE YOU IMPROVING? HOW DO YOU KNOW?

Metrics is a fancy word that means "a unit of evaluation, usually a number, that is used to measure progress toward a goal." Mastering the strategies and tactics outlined in this book will help you, your teams, and your organization be successful. They get precise — week by week, day by day, moment by moment — about how close they are to attaining what they want.

Finding the right way to measure your progress and then actually measuring it consistently is an essential part of the formula for personal success. To master that formula, you begin by understanding two critical points:

> ▶ First, if you can't measure it, you can't manage it. (That's true whether you're managing yourself

or other people. Management is an ongoing task and learning how to be an effective manager is a superpower.

▶ And second, only the stuff that gets measured gets rewarded.

It's not enough to have a clear vision of what success looks like. You must have clear *performance indicators* that tell you if you're getting closer to or further away from your goal.

The same is true whether you're a business owner or executive. You don't go broke making a profit. Measuring business success can be your net profit, stock price, market share, culture rating, or your Net Promoter Score (NPS). I'm sure you've seen the surveys; "On a scale of zero to 10 with 10 being the best, how likely is it that you would refer us to a friend or colleague?" The survey results mean those that rate 1–6 are less likely to shop and may leave negative reviews, 7-8 may refer if asked, and 9-10 are advocates. I had measurements for production schedules, quality control, number of sales calls and conversions, performance metrics between my painting crews, and routine financial reports. These *metrics* gave me consistent feedback on my progress toward success.

FLEX YOUR KPI MUSCLE

In business situations, the term *key performance indicators* (KPI) represent the quantifiable measurements agreed to beforehand that reflect the critical success factors of an organization. They differ depending on the organization. For personal use, you can identify what factors you're going to measure, how and when, and add them to your MAP.

Taking action on your mighty action plan without identifying the most important performance indicators that you're going to measure is a little like pointing yourself in a direction and then driving across the country blindfolded. You

CHAPTER SIXTEEN: THE POWER TO PIVOT

may start out with all kinds of confidence that you're headed west, from New York to San Francisco...but if you don't find a way to keep your eyes open along the way, watch the road signs, check your gauges, and track your progress toward your goal, you're not likely to make it to your destination.

Performance indicators are analogous to the road signs along the way that allow you to figure out how many miles you've traveled and in which direction. They tell you whether you're on or off track, getting closer to San Francisco as you drive (as opposed to, say, New Orleans), and they give you some sense of when you can expect to arrive. There's a reason you don't just get in the car and start driving in what feels like a westerly direction. There must be a process that you observe and measure along the way, a marker you use to evaluate whether the activity you're engaged in is working.

How you define *working,* specifically, is up to you. *Working* could mean that whatever you're doing is getting you closer to earning a half-million dollars in personal income in the next calendar year. Or it could mean you're closer to losing 30 pounds. It could mean you're closer to delivering a product with zero defects or to winning a 10-out-of-10 rating in terms of customer satisfaction from your clients. But whatever it is, confirm that the activity you've chosen to invest time, energy, effort, and attention in is delivering the outcome you want. Figure out whether you're making *measurable progress* on what's most important to you and your team. I'm sorry to dumb this down for you, but I want you to eliminate any excuses you have for not achieving your full potential.

Without key performance indicators to monitor, you could easily be wasting your time and energy. So, what are the key performance indicators you're going to keep track of? What activity can you count and record over time that correlates strongly with the attainment of *your* goal? Don't be scared of that word *correlate*. All it means is that whenever you take small steps, over time, you naturally move closer to delivering a bigger result — the result you want.

For example, suppose you're a salesperson and your goal is to earn a half-million dollars in income this year. In that case, your performance on that goal might be connected to the number of times you're able to set up an appointment with a qualified new prospect. That'll have a strong correlation with your ability to generate the income you want.

On the personal side, if it's a weight loss goal you're pursuing, one KPI you and your physician might come up with is a measure of how much time you spend exercising and the results of that exercise activity. (For instance: Did your heart rate go up? By how much? For how long?)

I own a training watch. It's a cool gadget that tracks multiple exercise activities, records the route with a multitude of measurements, and tracks my heart rate, calories, and exercise times. When I'm done exercising, I can upload the data and replay the route, along with analyzing my performance. Over time, I've seen my performance on repeated routes go up, and my average heart rate go down, showing me that I'm getting stronger, with more endurance.

In the business sector, the metrics are your financial statements, your income statement, balance sheet, sales reports, conversion percentages, ratios, and the like. If you're in management, you might monitor the number of hours spent on a project and the productivity of those hours. If it's manufacturing, you might look at cycle time, which is the total time required to get from the beginning to the end of the process, as defined by the manufacturer and the customer. (Cycle time includes both process time and delay time.) A business that operates without KPIs is like driving your car on the freeway with all the windows painted black and no gauges. You are certain to crash and burn.

The point is to know what your metrics are in advance. What does success look like? There's no excuse for not knowing. If you don't know, I encourage you to find out. And even if you do know (or think you do), keep monitoring, testing, and adjusting to improve your performance.

Selling is the classic example of how important metrics can be and how direct and powerful the connections are between activity and the result. Once you make those connections, you have a process you can follow. For great salespeople, it's all about following the process and understanding your own numbers. All you really need to know is how many sales calls you made and, out of those calls, how many relationships you built and what appointments you set. Out of those appointments, how many qualified leads did you get? Out of those qualified leads, which ones went through the first step of the introduction? You keep it up over time, you take those successive steps along the way, and eventually, you find the metrics become part of your routine.

CHAPTER 16 KEY CONCEPTS:

- Use metrics to measure success
- Practice a successful mindset
- Study your Key Performance Indicators

ACTION STEPS:

1. What are you measuring?

2. What are the key performance indicators you're going to keep track of?

3. What is your most important Key Performance Indicator?

4. What adjustments do you want to make to improve your performance?

5. What activity can you count and record over time that correlates strongly with the attainment of your goal?

CHAPTER SEVENTEEN:
SUPERPOWERED REFLEXES

We all need course corrections, feedback loops and people to help call us on our crap. As Albert Einstein said, "continuing to do the same thing over and over again and expecting a different result is the definition of insanity."

So, the question for any true superhero is: Are you willing to course-correct? Are you willing to notice whether you are getting closer to what you want and make minor or major shifts in your actions to achieve your goals? And here's a question that's just as critical: Are these adjustments consciously designed to keep you on course or distractions that move you further away from reaching your goals?

Let's take improving marketing conversions as an example. One of the key components in analyzing whether an advertisement or campaign is working is to use the following formula: test, track, modify, repeat. It's an excellent formula for advertising, and it's a great tool for life, too.

Here's the process. First, you establish a baseline metric, also called a control, and then perform a test. This could be an A/B split test of two website landing pages with different headlines, so you can track which version of the landing page performs the best. Once you've identified which page pulls the best result, that becomes your new A page (or control page) that you measure against. Then you modify one element on page B and repeat the A/B split test. If you pay attention and control the variables, you can know for sure — not just have a feeling, but have absolute certainty — about which works better, A or B.

This approach holds true to help increase marketing performance. It's also a solid framework for making course corrections for any goal or objective in life. You test, and then you track your performance over a period of time, modify your course, and continue on your journey.

So how does this principle apply to a personal goal? Let's use me as an example: I'm often categorized as a "driver" type personality. I've been self-employed almost my entire life. I believe I have majority control over my own environment. I set and follow rules, but I'm also open to changing them. I'm very opinionated, but I believe that I always discover better ways to learn, improve, and grow. The more I've learned over time, the more I know there is always ways to better my best. And so do you, or you wouldn't be in Chapter 17 of this book.

Now, my management style in the early years of my business operations was strictly commanding and controlling — if someone didn't do something the way I wanted it done or thought it should be done, I was the first person to say, "Hey, what the hell? This isn't right. We've got to fix this." Often, I came on way too strong.

This method was not effective and led to issues throughout the organization including culture, communication, and reduced employee retention. What was the one common denominator? Who was always at the scene of the crime?

Well, unfortunately, that would be me. I was driving people away who were trying to help, but at that time, I wasn't consciously open to their help. Wanting, no, *needing* to make changes, it was time to make serious course corrections. I started by taking full responsibility for my results. It began by being open-minded and coachable.

With the improved mindset, I was more open to hearing and understanding the insights from leadership & management books, courses, and topical experts. I started testing new strategies, tracking the performance, and making improvements from feedback to get better results.

Here's an example of that A/B split test where the B eventually became my A: Several years ago, a client called complaining that the flyers we designed and printed for her event hadn't reached the hotel yet. I checked with my shipping manager to track the shipment and get proof of delivery. I said, "Jim, did you send it 2nd-day air, and did you track the package?" He said, "Sorry, Ford. I thought I sent it out 2nd-day air, but the default shipping method is ground, and it shipped out ground, so it will not get to the hotel in time for the event." He had a terrified look on his face and clearly was concerned about how I would react. Why? Well, for one, the flyers were not going to get there in time, and now we have a problem. And two, Jim may have seen me overreact to similar situations in the past. Who knows?

This time around, though, I said, "Jim, it's no problem — just call the local FedEx Kinko's and send them a new PDF file so they can print them and get them to the client on time. It'll just cost us a little bit of money."

He came back to me and told me that it was going to end up costing $695 to have them printed, and I said, "Well, we've got to take care of the client, so just do it, and next time please double-check your work."

Later, after arranging for the reprinting and delivery of the flyers, Jim came into my office and said, "I just really want to thank you for how you handled that situation. I was really expecting you to be very upset with me and angry." I told him, "You know, mistakes happen, but my question to you is, did you learn from it?" He said yes, and I believe he did.

So again, through the years of the mistakes I've made and continue to make, I've become a little wiser. From a personal standpoint, I'm constantly looking at my baseline. What behavior can I test today to see improved results? What B page can I test against my current A page?

WHAT MIGHT WORK BETTER?

Once I had a very cynical employee who took an extremely negative approach to just about everything she did. One day I sat her down and said, "Look, I realize that cynicism is a strategy you use to protect yourself, I understand it, and we don't need to get into it. I don't want to psychoanalyze you but, for the next couple of days, I want you to practice smiling. When you go into meetings, instead of having your head down, instead of making snide remarks, just smile...and at the end of the week, let's see whether you've gotten better results or better performance. Are you willing to give that a try?"

She was. She changed her strategy, and she found a B that worked better than her A. She was able to see the feedback from everybody else she was working with. Now the team's happier, she's happier, her results are better, and she learned a new skill. So how can we be sure that it's the smiling that changed the outcome? Or how can I correct for any other variable that may have caused the change?

This is where we need to be sure to take your strategy to your Hero Handbook. You need to document exactly what you're going to do and what you're changing, and then keep track of your results. In direct response marketing, you don't want to change more than one element at a time because otherwise, you won't know what changed the result.

As a practical matter, when you are planning the new pages you want to test in your life, you're probably going to want to change only one thing at a time and use that change as the strategy you're keeping an eye on. That's what worked for me.

These are all just tools in your toolbox. My outcome with this book is for you to go to your toolbox and have more than a hammer. As we've all heard, if the only tool you have is a hammer, then every problem you run into looks like a nail.

REACTIVE OR ADAPTIVE?

There are two approaches to life we all should consider: reactive or adaptive. A reactive strategy is typical of people who are very set in their ways and constantly reacting to situations the same way. An adaptive strategy is one where the person incorporates new feedback, events, and viewpoints. I've noticed over the years that the growth potential of any team or organization is usually determined by the person at the top, not by the rest of the enterprise. If that person at the top is primarily reactive, the growth potential is low. If the leader is primarily adaptive, the growth potential is high.

I was a very reactive person in the earlier part of my life — I interrupted people, I didn't listen very well, and I still struggle with this at times. My operations manager used to say, "Are you listening to me? Or are you just waiting for your turn to talk?" I've learned that being reactive was a tool for me, and it was able to get me a certain level of success in some ventures, but not in the long run.

Being adaptive has proved a much better and wiser strategy for me. To be adaptive to the situation — for instance, dealing with the problem with the flyers that I mentioned — is a sign of emotional intelligence. It's one of the proudest achievements in my life. I wasn't adaptive at all in my 20s and 30s. Creative and innovative, yes, but not very adaptive in my attitude or opinions. I'm more adaptive now, which means my entire organization's potential is higher.

The point is that you should learn to diagnose the situation before you prescribe a solution, and you have to make sure that you're getting all the facts.

Here's an example of what I mean. Recently, I had lunch with Jeffrey Hayzlett, who wrote a book called *Running the Gauntlet*. Jeffrey is a global business celebrity and former Fortune 100 C-suite executive. He asked me whether I knew a specific PR person at the same conference where we were both speaking in Las Vegas. (We'll call the PR guy John.) John was at the networking event. John had approached Jeffrey by saying, "Hey, I'd like to spend 10 minutes with you and show you some ideas for taking your business to the next level."

The problem was that's the same pitch this guy has thrown at a thousand other speakers who aren't in Jeffrey's league. John had absolutely no idea who he was talking to. Jeffrey is already a TV producer, he already has multiple TV shows, he was on *The Celebrity Apprentice* with Donald Trump, and he is a best-selling author. How the heck is John going to take Jeffrey's business to the next level if he doesn't even know who he's talking to? If you ran into Paul McCartney, didn't recognize him, and told him you were ready to help him learn how to write a hit song, what kind of response do you think you'd get?

John took a completely reactive approach. He pitched Jeffrey before he had asked questions, before he had any understanding of the person he was dealing with. Even though he had made no effort to fill in any of those blanks, he jumped in wholly unprepared and proposed a solution. By doing that, he completely damaged his reputation with this (important) prospect. Jeffrey now thinks he's an idiot and will never hire him.

Let me repeat: Diagnose first before you jump to conclusions or attempt to offer advice. You need to have course correction. You need to make sure that you're paying attention to what the marketplace says and what the feedback is about you, minute by minute, day by day, year-round.

When you keep getting the same feedback from different sources, that's a sign that you need to do some more work in this area. If everyone around you tells you that you're difficult to work with, the problem probably isn't that everyone is out to get you. The problem likely is that you're difficult to work with and need to look at what you can change in your communication. In my case, everyone kept telling me, "Hey, you're not listening; you never let me finish." Now I'm in a mode where I'm working on implementing new strategies. I'm asking myself: What do I need to differently here? Do I need to stop and count to 10? Do I need to bring someone else into the conversation? Do I have to pause and find some new resources to learn new skills that will allow me to be better at whatever it is I want to accomplish?

The only way to know if what you're doing works is to *test it!*

The only way to know if you're getting the results you want is to *track it!* (Watch your metrics!)

The only way to avoid insanity is to *modify it!* Tweak it, make an adjustment, course-correct, or change so that you can expect a different result.

Then *repeat it!* Repeat it with the modifications you've made and start the whole process all over again.

This process of making course corrections allows you to put all your superpowers into action at full strength.

So don't skip this part! This is the step that will have to be repeated over and over and over again until you successfully reach your goals. This is the process that every great individual achiever, and every great company, has followed to make breakthroughs, dominate markets, and capture the imagination of consumers.

CHAPTER 17 KEY CONCEPTS:

- Take responsibility for the results in your life.
- Success Formula:
  - ▶ Test
  - ▶ Track
  - ▶ Modify
  - ▶ Repeat

ACTION STEPS:

1. What process are you testing right now?

2. How are you tracking your results?

3. What modifications will you make?

4. When will you repeat the process to see whether it works better than what you were doing before?

CHAPTER EIGHTEEN:
CREATING YOUR CAST OF CHARACTERS

WHO IS RUNNING the store? Who is in charge of reaching your team's goals? Management doesn't necessarily mean doing the work, but it does mean keeping an eye on what's happening, helping as needed, giving guidance and insights, and keeping people on task to get results. That means daily accountability, weekly accountability, monthly accountability, and annual accountability.

One mistake a lot of managers make is that they think they are looking at a KPI when in fact, they're looking at a target. For instance, if I'm a manager of a sales team and the only metric I measure is whether a sale closes — if the only question I ask is, "Did we get the deal done or didn't we?"— then I am ignoring every other potential metric before that closed deal. That's too bad, because measuring the metrics earlier in the process would have given my team the opportunity to affect their outcomes.

Of course, some people like to talk a lot about improving a team's closing skills, but the reality is that success in sales is much more likely to correlate with other activities that come long before the close. My point is that it's not only like that in the world of sales. It's like that just about everywhere.

A more effective manager won't wait until the sales team is hurtling toward the end of the quarter to tell them what they already know: They need to reach the finish line on time.

I like to tell managers a saying I learned from my friend Dan Burrus, author of *Flash Foresight:* Sometimes the problem isn't the problem. Here's what I mean by that. If I have water all over my floor and I wipe it up, I can talk myself into thinking I'm solving the problem, but in reality, the cracks in the wall that allow the water to leak in are the real problem. The key performance indicators have to be set at specific stages so that you really can evaluate what's causing (or preventing) forward progress. This has an impact on your team's effort, your tracking of that effort, and if the effort is paying off.

Of course, you may decide — for cash flow reasons, say — that it's important to you to know how much business your salespeople close every day. You may choose to look at that figure closely, and you may even assess daily how much closed business has actually come through compared to how much you expected...but if you don't like the number you see, then guess what? *The problem is not the problem.* You weren't monitoring the right number. You were looking at the outcome, not at what made it possible. What you want is information about whether the process worked so you can intervene and adjust the course if necessary. That means identifying a different process for tracking how your team is doing.

Finding the right KPI to manage your team is likely to be an ongoing challenge, even for an experienced manager. A lot depends on the individual goals of the team members who report to you, their level of career maturity, and the goals you and the team are responsible for reaching. It's a balancing act.

CHAPTER EIGHTEEN: CREATING YOUR CAST OF CHARACTERS

If the KPI is too complicated, people won't pay attention to it, but if it's not detailed, you're not going to get enough data to know whether your process is working.

Here's a list of some commonly used KPIs for teams with sales responsibility:

- ▶ Total number of prospecting calls made in a given period.
- ▶ Total number of initial appointments set in a given period.
- ▶ Amount of face time spent with prospects in a given period.
- ▶ Amount of face time spent with customers in a given period.
- ▶ Percentage of income from returning customers in a given period.
- ▶ Customer attrition rate in a given period. (Obviously, the lower it is, the more effective your sales and service process.)

Take the example of someone's website. You should manage that with the right metrics, too. The website owner may say, "Well, I really don't know what my website is doing!" or "My website's doing great!" unless they look at the website analytics and know how many first-time and repeat visitors there were, how many pages they visited, how many minutes they spent on the website, and the conversion percentages from specific action steps, then they really don't know much. What did your website visitors do? Did they sign up, opt-in, download content, request more information, complete a form, or buy a product? Measuring your success and defining what success looks like is the first step. Then, you want to put in the milestones and the benchmarks to measure your success and make corrective course changes.

CHAPTER 18 KEY CONCEPTS:

- Sometimes the problem isn't the problem
- Accountability
- Manage your metrics

ACTION STEPS:

What are you and your team accountable for on a daily basis?

1. On a weekly basis?

2. On a monthly basis?

3. On a quarterly basis?

4. On an annual basis?

PART 6:
REWARD

CHAPTER NINETEEN:
CELEBRATE YOUR WINS

THE LAST STEP in the superhero journey is the simplest, but it isn't easy for some people.

Are you waiting until you arrive at your final destination to celebrate your success? Do you realize that every small step along the way that is moving you toward your ultimate goal is a reason to celebrate?

Keep your long-term outcome in mind but set some benchmarks along the way to give you and your team cause to celebrate. Learning to enjoy the ride — and celebrate successes both large and small — can help you live in an attitude of gratitude.

BENEFITS OF ACKNOWLEDGING YOUR SUCCESSES

When you take the time to celebrate, you increase the positive neural pathways in your brain. This helps increase your motivation and helps you to develop a positive attitude. It reinforces your desired behaviors and makes it more likely that you'll take meaningful action toward your goals. To celebrate, reflect on your accomplishment, which gives you time to review where you are, what you've done, and where you want to go. You don't have to wait until you've reached the big goal to celebrate. In fact, I suggest you set up both big and small celebrations. Remember, each small step is a move in the right direction.

CELEBRATE THE SMALL STEPS

Your celebration doesn't need to be a big deal. It can be an activity you do by yourself or share with other people. The important part is that it makes you feel good and conditions positive responses for your accomplishment.

Here are a few great ways to celebrate your success:

- ▶ Go to a day spa.
- ▶ Take a vacation.
- ▶ Go shopping.
- ▶ Write a blog post.
- ▶ Play a musical instrument.
- ▶ Take a walk in the park.
- ▶ Read a fiction book.
- ▶ Connect with your friends.
- ▶ Take dance lessons.
- ▶ Capture the moment with photos.
- ▶ Record and post a video to YouTube.
- ▶ Pay to get your house cleaned.
- ▶ Buy flowers.
- ▶ Go for a run.
- ▶ Walk your dog.
- ▶ Send thank-you cards to everyone who supported you.
- ▶ Tell the media about it.

CHAPTER NINETEEN: CELEBRATE YOUR WINS

- ▶ Go out to a movie.
- ▶ Spend the day with your family.
- ▶ Go to a concert or play.
- ▶ Attend a sporting event.
- ▶ Tweet your accomplishment.
- ▶ Listen to the radio.
- ▶ Take a nap.
- ▶ Go out dancing.
- ▶ Spend a day in total silence.
- ▶ Go to the gym.
- ▶ Have a party.
- ▶ Write in your Hero Handbook.

Celebrating your success is much more than just telling other people about it. It's recognizing any progress on your journey toward your goals. If all you ever do is focus on the negative or the problems in your life and ignore the positive, this will undoubtedly derail your dreams and motivation to succeed. Focusing only on the negative and not rewarding yourself for the positive will chip away at your self-confidence. Stop and ask yourself, "What are three things I did right today?"

TAKE TIME TO SMELL THE ROSES

In the late 1990s, I was presenting to popular public seminar companies. This involved being on the road for three weeks of each month and traveling around the globe. I would fly out on a Sunday night, present on Monday from 9 a.m. to 4 p.m., and then drive to the next event city. I would repeat that process each day and fly home on Friday night. I did this for over three years and presented hundreds of full-day and multiday programs on various business-related and personal growth topics. My friends thought I had a glamorous life, but I mainly saw airports and hotel meeting rooms.

Looking back, I should have taken time to smell the roses and explore more of my surroundings. I didn't. I presented, packed up, drove to the next hotel, ate room service, watched a movie in the room, and then repeated the process. It's a shame I didn't take the time to get to know any of the attendees or appreciate the successes along the way. I certainly didn't celebrate the small steps along the way. My health suffered because I wasn't working out. My relationships at home suffered because I wasn't there. I was pretty much a speaking robot focusing on that one week a month between speaking tours.

We always have a choice, and I knew that it was time to make some serious choices. My first decision was to celebrate that I knew I needed to change. My second decision was to revisit my roles and goals and what I wanted in my life. I recognized that I needed to focus more on the moment and celebrate my successes each day. My focus changed from giving great presentations to connecting with the audiences to make a lasting impact. I took the time to pursue other revenue channels, develop more training resources, and ultimately spent less time on the road. I resigned from the public seminar company as a contract trainer and grew my keynote speaking and consulting business. I wrote in my journal more and took more pictures and videos of the people and places around me. Each night before I went to sleep, I celebrated what I had learned, the people I had communicated with, and my accomplishments.

THE POWER OF EFFORT

CHAPTER NINETEEN: CELEBRATE YOUR WINS

My wife is a Pilates instructor who certifies other Pilates teachers. She tells her clients the story of fitness pioneer Joseph Pilates celebrating "champagne moments" with his clients. When they finally nailed an exercise or met a goal, Joseph would stop all activity in the studio and pop a cork on a bottle of champagne. Everyone would toast to their success — a celebration of achievement. I'm not suggesting you drink alcohol as a celebration, but I do want you to give yourself positive rewards regularly.

Share your superpower of appreciation with those around you who are supporting the achievement of your goals. Share a copy of *Superpower!* with someone you care about.

As you start the journey to develop your superpowers, I hope this book has given you ideas to improve one or more areas of your life. Even more, I hope the processes and action steps in this book will transform your results.

CHAPTER 19 KEY CONCEPTS:

Acknowledge your success in all areas of focus.

List Five Ways You Can Celebrate Your Successes

1. _____

2. _____

3. _____

4. _____

5. _____

What are the smaller benchmarks along the way that you will be able to celebrate, knowing that you're heading in the right direction to achieve your goals?

What will you do to celebrate the (significant!) benchmark of completing this book?

CHAPTER TWENTY:
POWERFUL RESULTS

I **SHARED AT THE** beginning of this book...there's always more to learn. Practice doesn't make perfect, practice makes improvement. All the ideas and insights you've learned won't help unless you take action to apply them. Your success depends on using the concepts in this book regularly – *practicing* this new knowledge, making adjustments as necessary, and putting your new superhero skills to work. It takes time and dedication. The process is powerful, and you'll be amazed at the renewed. It takes time and dedication. The process is powerful, and you'll be amazed at the renewed results you can accomplish for yourself and your business.

Most of all, it takes:

Rethinking your current mindset to unlock your superpowers and focus on success...

Reframing by getting clear on what you want to do, be, have, or become...

Refocusing on superpowered instinct and developing your be amazed at the renewed results you can accomplish for yourself and your business.Most of all, it takes:

185

Rethinking your current mindset to unlock your superpowers and focus on success...

Reigniting your mission by creating your mind MAP...

Reflecting on the changes and powerful progress you've made, and...

Rewarding your hard work by setting mini-goals and then *celebrating* them!

And when you think about it, isn't that what superpower is all about? You *can* think, act, and perform like no one else no one else to get the results you want in business, leadership, and life, because you have Superpowers.

ABOUT THE AUTHOR

THE BUSINESS GROWTH ACCELERATOR

Ford Saeks is more than a hall of fame keynote speaker, he's a research-based thought leader. An engine. An expert. An idea man and marketing machine. He helps businesses not by talking at them about success, but by talking them through the steps to get there.

Ford started his first business at 15 years old and has been succeeding ever since. He has redefined the formula for business growth. His efforts have helped companies generate more than $1 billion in sales worldwide.

From start-ups to Fortune 500s, Saeks is widely recognized as a business growth expert. With over 30 years of experience (ranging from retail to wholesale), he has founded more than ten companies, authored four books, secured three U.S. patents, and earned numerous industry awards.

SKYROCKET RESULTS

In his popular keynotes or in his private consultations, Ford helps businesses find a way forward. That means first identifying what it is that is holding them back. There is a gap between where they want to be and where they are now. Once business owners are clear on their gap and put the right mindset, strategies, and tactics into place, the results are extraordinary. They see radical growth in the business.

TAKE A PAGE OUT OF FORD'S BOOK(S)

Ford Saeks is an author with your success in mind. His books offer expert advice, action steps and other useful takeaways for the motivated entrepreneur, business owner, CEO, marketing professional, and manager.

MOVER, SHAKER, RAINMAKER

Tenacity and innovation are what fuel this revenue-generating powerhouse. From grassroots to Google, Ford provides his clients with fresh perspectives and doable tactics to resolve marketing, operations, and growth challenges.

As President and CEO of Prime Concepts Group, Inc., a creative marketing agency, Ford specializes in helping businesses attract loyal and repeat buyers, monetize social media, and ignite creativity. Visit PrimeConcepts.com

CONNECT WITH FORD ONLINE

Discover more about Ford Saeks at **ProfitRichResults.com**

SOCIAL MEDIA

FORDIFY™
MARKETING. SALES. CUSTOMER EXPERIENCE. LEADERSHIP.

SUBSCRIBE TO FORD'S YOUTUBE CHANNEL
Fordify.TV

SUPERPOWER!

FIRED UP IS NICE, FUELED UP IS BETTER

Elevate PERFORMANCE
Accelerate GROWTH
Generate PROFITS

Watch Trailer

FORD SAEKS
BUSINESS GROWTH ACCELERATOR

BRIDGE THE GAP, GROW YOUR BUSINESS.

Think about this... No matter where you're at now, there is someplace you want to go with the growth and success of your business. In every situation, there is a gap and people feel that gap is truly unique to them.

Organizations are dealing with...

- ✓ Increased Competition
- ✓ Struggling to Retain Top Talent
- ✓ Disruption From Many Directions

Ford has worked with top brands throughout the world, small and large, from start-ups to billion-dollar brands, helping them produce higher levels of personal and professional success.

THE GAP ALWAYS COMES DOWN TO ONE OR MORE OF THESE THREE AREAS: Mindset   Strategy   Tactics

Once you are clear on the gap and put the right mindset, strategies, and tactics into place, the results are extraordinary. **The Accelerated Growth System™** uncovers the path and the processes to drive exponential growth year after year.

FORD'S MOST REQUESTED PRESENTATIONS:

Business Growth Acceleration
Maximize Your Findability, Accountability, and Profitability

Remarkable Customer Engagement
Creating a Customer-Centric Culture That Drives Repeat & Referral Sales

Winning Workplace Strategies
How To Find, Engage, & Retain Top Talent

Superpower Success
Unleash Your Inner Superhero To Bust Through Barriers & Ignite High Performance

Innovative Marketing Mastery
Leveraging Your Brand To Build Relationships & Skyrocket Your Sales

Your Digital Footprint Needs New Shoes
Driving Traffic and Building Your Online Reputation to Grow Your Business

SUPERPOWER!

MOVE FORWARD...
FASTER

ON-STAGE   ON-SCREEN   ON-DEMAND

4 Reasons Why Brands Love Working with Ford

1. Ford knows how important it is to anticipate future trends, adapt to changing buyer behaviors and help others seize opportunities.

2. His presentations are high-energy, topical, and engaging. They're perfect for participants in different roles and levels of experiences.

3. Your audience members will gain fresh insights, equipped with actionable takeaways that are in alignment with your event outcomes.

4. As the opening keynote speaker, he will kick off your conference with a bang. As the closing keynote speaker, he will ensure your attendees leave with a prioritized massive action plan.

About Ford Saeks
Business Growth Accelerator

- Hall of Fame Keynote Speaker
- Business Consultant
- Successful Entrepreneur
- Research-Based Thought Leader
- Author of 5 business books
- 1,500+ Keynotes Delivered Globally
- Founder of 3 Multi-Million Dollar Companies
- Inventor & Multiple Patent Holder
- Avid Gravel Cyclist

Just a few of the many
brands that trust Ford to help accelerate their results

SPEAKER PACKET

YOUR GUIDE TO GROWTH

Meeting planners love Ford Saeks because he exceeds expectations with customized presentations that are on-target, on-theme, and value-added.

U.S. LAWNS
"If we stopped our event today on day one, we've already got a wealth of knowledge and content we can take home and apply, and it's been a success already."
— Ben Lively, Sales Coach, **U.S. Lawns**

GOLD'S GYM
"Our franchisees valued Ford's **great content and dynamic delivery style**—he did his homework and really understood our brand and our franchisee's challenges."
— Bridget Sypolt, Director of Meetings, **Gold's Gym International**

LIBERTY TAX
"Ford Saeks was our guest speaker at a recent Area Developer Retreat and our attendees absolutely LOVED him! His material was **'spot-on' for what we wanted delivered** and his actionable **take-aways truly resonated with our team**."
— Karen Halman, Director of Training, **Liberty Tax**

RIA
"We booked Ford for our national convention and hoped he'd live up to all the hype we'd heard. He EXCEEDED the hype. His keynote knocked it out-of-the-park and his break-out session was full to overflowing—not only with attendees, but with usable, salient, practical ideas for our members' businesses."
— Cynthia Hereth, Meeting Planner, **Restoration Industry Association (RIA)**

BANK OF AMERICA
"Ford put much effort into understanding our company and developing a program that would successfully meet our objectives. **His attention to detail and extensive preparation were impressive**, and we look forward to inviting him back in the future."

BEST SELLING AUTHOR ON BUSINESS GROWTH

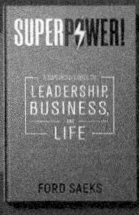

- SUPERPOWER! A Superhero's Guide to Leadership, Business, and Life — FORD SAEKS
- ACCELERATE: A Franchisee's Guide to Dominate Local Markets and Increase Sustainable Sales — FORD SAEKS
- PROFIT-RICH MARKETING: Proven Strategies to Help You Grow Your Business — Ford Saeks

Let's Discuss Your Needs for Your Next Conference, Training, or Event.

Call/Text **(316) 207-6718** or
Visit **ProfitRichResults.com**

Watch Trailer

193

WATCH FORD'S SPEAKER TRAILER

DOWNLOAD THE HERO HANDBOOK

Superpowerbook.com/downloads

The Hero Handbook will help you take personal accountability for your success. That's where all the power and responsibility is — within you.

Read each chapter of Superpower!, then leverage the exercises found in this handbook to further rethink, reframe, refocus, and reignite your leadership, your business, your life. The actions you take here are the first steps in your journey.

INDEX

A

ABC Method 112
accountability vii, ix, 34, 131, 132, 136, 137, 139, 149, 173, 195
action steps 2, 14, 33, 88, 122, 175, 183, 188
adaptive 167
analogy 131
approach iii, 26, 130, 140, 164, 166, 168
apps 86, 157
attitude 11, 25, 38, 39, 49, 68, 140, 141, 149, 168, 179

B

Batman 9, 10, 73, 74, 76, 77
belief system 26
Beowulf 10
bicycle 42, 44, 45, 47, 55
Black Panther 10
books vi, 1, 2, 10, 31, 36, 63, 67, 76, 77, 90, 136, 165, 187, 188
brain 42, 57, 76, 81, 93, 97, 117, 126, 179
brainstorming 82, 83, 85
Brown, Les 99
Bryant Avenue Paint 30
Burrus, Dan 174
business i, vii, 1, 3, 8, 9, 10, 25, 26, 27, 30, 31, 35, 36, 39, 41, 43, 44, 46, 47, 48, 53, 54, 55, 57, 58, 63, 64, 68, 74, 76, 77, 78, 80, 82, 85, 89, 91, 100, 102, 117, 118, 119, 123, 128, 129, 136, 137, 138, 140, 141, 148, 155, 156, 158, 160, 164, 168, 174, 182, 187, 188, 195
Business Growth Expert 187
Buzan, Tony 85

C

can-do attitude 25, 38, 49, 140

can't-do attitude 28, 31, 122
career 10, 111, 136, 146, 174
Carnegie, Andrew 136
Cathcart, Jim iii
celebrate 184
cell phone 27, 45, 100, 108, 109, 110, 111, 123, 131, 157
change ii, 8, 11, 34, 37, 68, 99, 105, 146, 147, 166, 167, 169, 182
child 25, 53
childlike 10
choices 31
client 8, 9, 118, 119, 131, 148, 165
Coaches 136
combination 26, 44, 57, 58
common sense 55, 136
community 121
concepts 1, 3, 87, 120
consciousness 12, 48, 49
consistent 67, 101, 158
corporate 40, 117
correlate 160, 173
course correction 169
creative 80, 82, 168
creativity 80, 84, 87, 188
critical thinking 92
critical thinking skills 2, 157
cross-train 81, 88
customer 7, 8, 9, 35, 38, 74, 77, 111, 155, 159, 160

cynicism 50, 166

D

Debolt, John 98
destination 64, 69, 110, 124, 159, 179
develop vii, 10, 13, 47, 50, 75, 76, 84, 97, 118, 119, 137, 155, 179, 182, 183
developing 49, 88, 89, 91

discipline 68
distraction 107, 110
download ix, 14, 195

E

Eberle, Bob 84
education 31
effort 182
Einstein, Albert 163
electronic vi
eliminate 49, 83, 102, 159
email 109, 110, 111, 130
embezzled 148
emotional intelligence 168
emotional survival 147
entrepreneur 2, 26, 27, 41, 136, 188
excuses 80
experience iii, 3, 8, 13, 26, 27, 28, 30, 55, 56, 74, 75, 77, 97, 98, 102, 120, 138, 145, 147, 148, 156, 187
experts 28

F

Facebook 12, 130
faith 9, 99
feedback 69, 122, 138, 139, 156, 157, 158, 163, 165, 166, 167, 169
Flash Foresight 174
floating swimwear 52
focus 34, 35, 41, 42, 44, 74, 75, 76, 78, 87, 109, 110, 111, 124, 130, 181, 182, 184
Ford, Henry 37, 156
Ford list 112

G

Gain Advantage 11, 12
GAME ON 11
Global Spectrum 123, 124
goal 2, 35, 65, 66, 68, 71, 75, 78, 112, 117, 118, 130, 132, 137, 157,

158, 159, 160, 162, 164, 179, 183
gratitude 150, 151
great leap forward 146
growth 1, 14, 31, 50, 77, 78, 82, 102, 136, 140, 167, 182, 187, 188
guide iii, 13
guidebook vii

H

handbook vii, 13, 195
Hayzlett, Jeffrey 168
health and fitness 12
Hero Handbook ix, 13, 14, 33, 50, 60, 86, 131, 151, 166, 195
High Point University i
Hill, Napoleon 142

I

I can 2, 25, 26, 27, 29, 31, 37, 42, 47, 56, 65, 79, 97, 112, 118, 124, 149, 160, 174
ideas i, 1, 2, 3, 13, 42, 55, 59, 60, 79, 80, 81, 82, 83, 84, 85, 87, 88, 101, 102, 104, 112, 118, 131, 137, 140, 168, 183
impact 11, 25, 34, 66, 174, 182
Improving 74, 157
infomercial 56, 57, 101
innovations 80
Instagram 12
instinct 99
intelligence 168
Interbike 44, 45
internet 27, 122, 139
interruptions 100, 111, 112, 114
intuition 97

J

job security 12, 75
Jobs, Steve 140
journal 33, 131, 182
journey 11

judgmental 137

K

key concepts 15, 33, 49, 60, 71, 78, 87, 92, 100, 104, 114, 126, 133, 142, 151, 162, 171, 176, 184
keynote speaker 1, 102, 187
key performance indicators 158, 159, 162, 174
Kindle vi, 77
KPI 158, 160, 173, 174, 175

L

landing page 164
leader iii, 3, 8, 66, 76, 136, 145, 167, 187
leadership vii, 1, 3, 10, 11, 48, 64, 80, 102, 117, 129, 136, 140, 165, 195
learned ADD 108, 112
Legacy Masters 136, 139
leveraging 129
life i, ii, iii, vii, 1, 2, 3, 7, 8, 10, 11, 12, 13, 25, 27, 28, 31, 34, 36, 37, 38, 40, 41, 42, 43, 48, 49, 52, 57, 63, 64, 65, 66, 67, 74, 75, 76, 80, 81, 82, 89, 98, 99, 100, 101, 102, 103, 104, 105, 111, 117, 118, 121, 123, 124, 125, 127, 135, 136, 137, 140, 141, 146, 147, 148, 149, 151, 152, 155, 156, 163, 164, 167, 168, 171, 181, 182, 183, 195
lifeline experience 145
lifestyle 39, 118
LinkedIn 77, 130, 139

M

management 127, 158, 173
manager 39, 54, 58, 83, 158, 165, 167, 173, 174, 188
MAP 117, 118, 120, 124, 126, 127, 158
marketing i, 28, 31, 44, 47, 53, 55, 58, 85, 87, 102, 118, 123, 124, 129, 131, 163, 164, 167, 187, 188
Mastermind Groups 137
McElveen-Hunter, Bonnie 25
measurable progress 159

mentor 65, 77, 135, 136, 137, 139, 140, 141
metrics 13, 69, 118, 122, 155, 158, 160, 161, 162, 169, 173, 175, 176
mind mapping 85, 86, 92, 117
mindset 1, 11, 26, 31, 33, 35, 37, 41, 42, 44, 68, 148, 157, 162, 165, 188
Mitchell, W. 11
Monetize Everything 11, 12
money 11, 12, 26, 27, 28, 30, 39, 45, 52, 54, 55, 56, 57, 64, 69, 79, 98, 120, 124, 128, 137, 155, 165
monotasking 107
multitasking 107, 109

N

negative 28, 43, 44, 49, 74, 90, 124, 145, 146, 147, 148, 158, 166, 181
Netflix 12, 50
numbers 69, 120, 161

O

opportunity 28, 36, 37, 45, 46, 47, 52, 54, 60, 99, 111, 124, 138, 173
Osborne, Alex 84
outcome 60, 65, 92, 118, 122, 159, 166, 167, 174, 179
outline 2, 85, 119
Overlook Nothing 11, 12

P

Palmer Heck, Jean 11
parking lot 110, 112
parking spaces 110
patents 64, 187
persistence 48
personal iii, vii, ix, 1, 3, 11, 12, 13, 31, 34, 36, 43, 50, 64, 71, 75, 78, 88, 110, 118, 121, 136, 138, 139, 140, 141, 156, 157, 158, 159, 160, 164, 166, 182, 195
personal accountability vii, ix, 34, 195
Pilates, Joseph 183
pivot 155

positive 2, 26, 29, 35, 36, 37, 42, 43, 47, 48, 49, 78, 90, 140, 141, 145, 146, 147, 149, 155, 179, 180, 181, 183
power iii, vii, ix, 10, 65, 99, 102, 129, 135, 138, 140, 141, 195
practice 83, 100, 104, 162
Prime Concepts Group vi, 3, 39, 102, 129, 188
Prime Concepts Group Press vi
priorities 33
problem 7, 41, 42, 44, 45, 57, 92, 107, 108, 111, 149, 150, 165, 167, 168, 169, 174, 176
profit vi, 74
progress 156
prospects 131, 175
prosperity 35, 49, 121
prosperity consciousness 12, 48, 49
Prosperity Consciousness Superpower 49

Q

Qubein, Dr. Nido R. i
question 37, 38, 57, 69, 111, 123, 132, 163, 166, 173

R

reactive 167
reality 55, 65, 68, 122, 173, 174
referral 128
refocus vii, 195
reframe vii, 195
reignite vii, 195
relationship 137, 142
resources 12, 36, 50, 76, 77, 110, 119, 120, 122, 128, 131, 139, 148, 169, 182
responsibility vii, ix, 127, 137, 165, 171, 175, 195
responsive anger 149
results ii, 2, 3, 11, 30, 31, 33, 34, 36, 50, 67, 74, 84, 100, 101, 102, 113, 114, 122, 128, 156, 158, 160, 165, 166, 167, 169, 171, 173, 183, 188
rethink vii, 195
Rohn, Jim 136
Running the Gauntlet 168

S

Saeks Painting and Light Construction 27
Sanborn, Mark ii, iii
SCAMPER Technique 84
Schwab, Charles M. 136
self iii, 11, 26, 28, 36, 43, 44, 47, 68, 89, 109, 128, 135, 149, 164, 181
self-esteem 68
Simple vs. Easy 127
simplicity 101
Sims, Steve 27, 45

skills vii, 2, 9, 12, 31, 38, 39, 75, 76, 77, 132, 140, 156, 157, 169, 173
smartphone 59, 86
snapshot 117, 145
social media 3, 118, 139, 188
solution 42, 52, 81, 86, 93, 168, 169
Speakers Roundtable 138
speed skating 97, 147
Spiderman 9, 135
spirituality 12
sports 123
strategic 2, 39, 82
strategies i, ii, vi, vii, 1, 2, 57, 58, 64, 101, 102, 118, 122, 127, 129, 136, 157, 165, 169, 188
strength 129, 169
substitute 84
success ii, iii, vii, ix, 1, 2, 10, 11, 12, 13, 25, 26, 31, 36, 38, 39, 58, 59, 64, 66, 71, 74, 76, 77, 78, 87, 89, 91, 101, 117, 118, 123, 124, 129, 136, 139, 140, 141, 155, 156, 157, 158, 161, 162, 167, 173, 175, 179, 180, 181, 183, 184, 187, 188, 195
Success Library 76, 77, 90
superhero 10, 11, 13, 25, 26, 31, 76, 135, 147, 163, 179
Superman 8, 9, 53, 135
Superpower i, ii, iii
Superpower Choices 31

Superpower Mindset 1
survival 89, 147

T

tactics ii, vii, 1, 101, 122, 127, 157, 188
Taylor, Jim 110
team iii, 3, 67, 74, 77, 82, 83, 84, 111, 112, 119, 123, 124, 129, 132, 147, 156, 159, 166, 167, 173, 174, 176, 179
technology 37, 39, 107, 108, 109, 129, 139
testing 57, 76, 161, 165, 171
Test, Track, Modify, Repeat 171
The Celebrity Apprentice 168
The Compound Effect 136
thought leaders 1
TikTok 12, 50
time management 127
tools vii, 28, 39, 77, 107, 108, 110, 123, 141, 151, 157, 167
Tough Talks for Tough Times 11
Toyota 11, 12
tracking 157, 165, 171, 174
Tracy, Brian i
trade shows 44, 58, 123
transformation 9, 135
transition 26
trust 97

V

value 7, 53, 63, 74, 75, 76, 77, 78, 79, 82, 102, 120, 128, 130
video 50, 119, 129, 141, 180

W

wealth 12, 48, 71, 122, 125
website 85, 112, 118, 164, 175
weight 118, 127, 128, 131, 157, 160
wins 179
Wonder Woman 9
work experience 26

working ii, 8, 11, 12, 30, 31, 57, 69, 101, 110, 114, 122, 148, 149, 156, 159, 163, 166, 169, 175, 182

Y

YouTube 77, 139, 180

CPSIA information can be obtained
at www.ICGtesting.com
Printed in the USA
JSHW062151180722
28243JS00007B/342